Discovering Sexuality That Will Satisfy You Both

Discovering Sexuality That Will Satisfy You Both

WHEN COUPLES WANT DIFFERING AMOUNTS AND DIFFERENT KINDS OF SEX

✦ ✦ ✦

Anne Stirling Hastings, Ph. D.

The Printed *Voice*

© 1993 Anne Stirling Hastings

Published by:
The Printed Voice
98 Main St., No. 538
Tiburon, CA 94920

Cover Design:
Kathy Warinner

Text Design:
Tori Hernandez

Library of Congress Cataloging-in-Publication Data

Hastings, Anne Stirling, 1943-
    Discovering sexuality that will satisfy you both : when couples
want differing amounts and different kinds of sex / Anne Stirling
Hastings.
        p.   cm.
    Includes bibliographical references.
    ISBN 0-9637891-1-2 : $9.95
    1. Sex. 2. Intimacy (Psychology) 3. Sex addiction.   I. Title.
HQ21.H3296   1993
    306.7--dc20   93-27301
                                                            CIP

First Printing, October 1993
Printed in the U.S.A. on acid-free paper
10 9 8 7 6 5 4 3 2 1

TABLE OF CONTENTS

ACKNOWLEDGMENTS

Laurie Harper approaches the work of agenting books with emotional and financial integrity, and a commitment to presenting information in a way that best serves all, including authors, publishers and readers. I appreciate her active model of my most cherished principles, as well as her support of my thinking and writing.

Leslie Keenan, my editor and publisher, brings her sense of integrity and commitment to the subversive nature of truth.

Rex Holt, my mate, feels no sacrifice when I write on beaches, on vacation, in restaurants and in bed. His needs sift together with mine, and mine with his—as in sex. Because this process is so natural I don't feel the emotion of appreciation. He isn't giving me a gift. Our relationship together is a gift I acknowledge.

The support of Jill Seipel and Louisa Turner has made my work life feel more sane, as has Cathy Rogers' accurate mirroring.

Those of you who come to me to work toward retrieving your sexuality, and who are willing to face the shame that must accompany deep healing, and who are willing to stay with painful feelings to get to the other side, and whose stories form the basis of this book—I embrace you.

If you would like information about classes, workshops, speeches or training for therapists, please drop me a note.

My address is:

> Integrity Resources
> P.O. Box 40083
> Bellevue, WA 98005

If you would like to share your experiences after reading this book, I would appreciate receiving them. Thanks.

In celebration of my life with

Rex Holt

who learns with me how to retrieve healthy sexual energy, and who, of course, wants the same kind and same amount of sex.

Introduction

Millions of people in recovery are going to work on their sexuality. Some identify themselves as recovering sex addicts, some as incest survivors and some simply know they are having sexual "problems." An exciting outcome of this massive energy expenditure is the opportunity to discover the real nature of sexuality. As these millions find out the truth—and live it—the world's sexuality will change.

In my work as a psychologist helping people who want to change their use of sexuality, I have encountered many couples who believed they differed in their desire for sex and their preferences for choice of sexual activities. In therapy, they discovered their differences resulted from childhood programming and the effects of our distorted culture. As I watched them strip away effects of the damage, I observed couples becoming more "compatible" with each other. As they became increasingly sensitive to their sexuality and that of their partner, sex evolved creatively on its own. My own experience in my second marriage has shown me that when we remove harmful past influences, sex takes on a different character. I have written this book from my developing understanding of the nature of sexuality. I offer it to those who are working with a partner to discover how to use this vital energy in ways that can bond them, enhance their lives together and create a natural, inside-out monogamy that is effortless.

My clients have shown me that the usual approach of behavioral sex therapists misleads people into thinking that more of our culture's distorted sex is good, and that anything "between consenting adults" is acceptable. There is an alternative. *Instead of grasping for outside stimulation to make sexual energy appear, it is possible to make room for a fresh, new sexuality to emerge from the inside.*

As the sexual recovery of individuals progresses, it is evolving into a movement lead by those who suffer from childhood sexual abuse memories or from sexual addiction. These people's pain is so great they are forced to scrap the old views of sexuality. The benefit for all of us is their discovery of a different kind of sexuality—a spiritual variety quite different from the intensity sex therapists promote.

With a cultural shift underway, we are more willing to examine the apparently different levels of sexual "interest" between partners. As a therapist, I see many couples who come to me because they differ over how much sex to have, what kind, where and when. As these individuals work together to explore their own sexuality and gradually abandon our culture's views, they discover that *the experience of differing sexual "needs" is only a creation of our culture.* Those who have been in sexual recovery for a time appreciate that a mechanical view of sex just doesn't make sense. Instead, they are learning that the "need" for sex has to do with the bonding of two people into a couple, in order to enhance their spiritual, intimate lives together.

To achieve this bonding, couples discover a new kind of sexuality that comes from the inside out. The old kind requires them to respond in ways they've learned from the culture, triggered by outside-in stimuli such as romance or provocative images in movies, on TV, in pornography and so on. The process I put forth in the chapters that follow will help couples to move away from their "differences." It involves unearthing hidden damage, the result of incest or other unhealthy relationships that occurred during childhood, or as a result of the dictates of our culture. I present specific approaches that allow shame to be stripped away from sex so you and your mate can discover that you desire the same frequency and kind of sex.

When couples can free themselves from unhealthy sex, the kind that promotes differences in partners, their sexual natures emerge in new and loving ways. As a result, couples find that the desire for sex is absurd when one's partner isn't interested. Sex becomes less appealing when one has to "seduce," or talk the other person into having it. Sex is also less appealing for the person who feels required to meet the "sexual needs" of another. Yet, to date, there has been nothing offered that shows people how to move toward healthy, spiritual sex. That is why I wrote this book.

In these pages I offer entirely new ways for couples to perceive sex. I describe how relationships can be an arena of healing for damage caused by sexual abuses in childhood and from our culture. I describe what sex might be like for those who can set aside attitudes created by our culture.

It is possible for all of us to discover the real nature of bonding, of loving sexual activity. As more and more of us know the truth we will influence our children and others around us. Eventually our culture will change and useful sexuality will be an integrated part of being human.

Chapter 1

The Frustration Of Differing Sexual "Needs"

Almost everyone has wanted sex and been turned down. It doesn't feel good. It also doesn't feel good to have a partner ask for sex when you're not inclined to respond. It feels even worse to agree to have sex when you don't want it.

These common situations turn into problems when they occur repeatedly. Resentments build on both sides, and marriages end because there is no resolution. These experiences are so painful they bring couples into therapy more than any other sexual issue. An initially small difference becomes intensified when the one who wants less sex wants even less when pressured, and the one who wants more wants even more when rejected.

Jackie and Bob came for therapy when she reached a point of exasperation because Bob didn't want to have sex with her. She believed he didn't love her. She also questioned if she was "sexy" enough to be attractive to him. As a result of their sexual conflicts, they developed complaints about each other that were insoluble because they didn't address the basic hurt.

When I met with Bob, I learned that he only felt sexual with women the first few times he had sex. After that, he would lose

5

interest. Even his sexual fantasies were of women he'd just met. Bob also felt more comfortable masturbating than making love with a real person. We discussed the possible roots of this sexual limitation, looking for the cause of his constraints.

We learned that Bob lived in hope of finding a magical sexual experience that would save him from his mundane, shame-filled existence. However, after his first or second time with a woman, she would fall from the pedestal, obviously not the goddess he was seeking. From then on, she would seem sexually repulsive, someone who wanted to consume him with her need instead of taking care of his. The disgust prevented him from getting an erection. Even heavy use of pornography did not help.

I have heard the stories of many people who are frustrated by a level of interest in sex that differs from their partner's. Women and men feel obligated to be sexual when their partner wants it, and those who want less than the partner feel guilty for setting limits.

Rea's husband was in therapy for his addiction to sex with prostitutes. He told me that his wife felt fine about their high frequency of sexual activity. Yet when Rea came to my women's support group, she told us he wanted too much sex. He also wanted her to wear "sexy" clothing to arouse him, which didn't feel comfortable to her. They hadn't yet reached the point of being able to talk about their differences after twenty years of marriage. Rea raged with the women, but went for weeks before she was able to tell her husband the truth. She had been a marital prostitute by having sex when she didn't want it for the "payment" of financial support and the status of being married.

Michael acted out sexually in his earlier years while drinking addictively. He had affairs with women who couldn't stand to be without him. At the same time he had only a moderate interest in sex with his first wife. Alcohol helped increase his arousal so he could have sex in order to prevent his wife from complaining. However, once he stopped drinking and entered recovery, he divorced his first wife and soon thereafter married a woman who was addicted to sex with him, just as his lovers had been. But now his "lover" lived with him and was in his bed every night. He soon found that he couldn't be aroused by her pursuit, and had to resort to injections in his penis to create erections. He hadn't dealt with his resentment, however, and sex became a battlefield for the marriage.

The story of Eileen, Michael's second wife, is also poignant. She grew up in a family where people were always leaving, either walking away or dying. She was exposed to sexualized "caring" as a child, and consequently she cross-wired love with sexual attention. When she felt lonely or very sad, she wanted to have sex in order to feel filled up again. When Michael was reluctant to provide this for her, she felt unloved by him, abandoned and deprived of what she called her "sexual expression." These two people had been in therapy, trying to reach compromises. The underlying issue of the real nature of sex had not been addressed, and so they could only feel frustrated. There was no "solution."

People who don't receive the sex they feel they need and deserve often feel rejected, abandoned and unloved. In addition, they feel deprived of a pleasure they were told they could have when they were married. Now finally married, they are still shamed for wanting sex.

Trina couldn't admit she was frightened when Monty wanted sex. She was terrified that she wasn't a "real" woman, and was perhaps asexual, if she didn't immediately respond to his overtures. She thought she should be like her mother who was always ready to respond to sexual energy, from her husband or anyone else who paid sexual attention to her. Trina wasn't aware there was a way to experience her sexuality that was different from her mother's approach to sex or her father's inhibitions regarding it. Neither choice seemed appealing. Because Trina felt shamed by her lack of interest, she shamed her husband for wanting sex. By making him look like the one who was wrong, she could avoid her own feelings.

Monty took on the shaming and felt like a defective person, which made him angry and demanding. Shame is painful, and he avoided his by turning on his wife, raging at her for not upholding her marital obligation. The cycle continued as she responded to his raging with further shaming, which encouraged his raging response. This situation continued until they were able to get help in understanding what they were doing.

Margaret and Steven were perfectly matched for a miserable sex life in their marriage. He whimpered his feelings of rejection when Margaret didn't want to have sex. She was repulsed by him, and refused sex even more. He blamed and criticized her, pushing until she "gave in" occasionally. When they did have sex, both felt closer for a few days, confirming to him that sex made the marriage better. But neither knew that Margaret had been sexually abused by her father in her early childhood. Once Margaret discovered that she had been required to take care of her father's needs—a role she was assigned in the family system—she could see the parallel with Steven's objection that she wasn't taking care of his needs. While she didn't want to have sex with a man who felt she must, at the same time we could see that the intensity of her reaction came from the past.

Lena felt betrayed when she returned home unexpectedly to find her husband masturbating to a video. He rarely had sex with her. He felt tremendous shame for choosing solitary release over sex with a woman.

Alecia was chagrined when, after saving intercourse until her wedding night, she found that her husband wasn't very interested in making love. He was also shocked to find that his wife didn't act like the prostitutes he had been with who went after him, fully expecting to be involved in the sexual exchange. After a few years of feeling like a failure for not being able to make love to his wife, he began to have affairs with women who were forbidden, and who wanted him intensely. Both were angry with each other for being inadequate sexual partners and spouses.

Hazel and her husband lived with simmering resentment. He wanted her to want sex so he could feel loved, but she felt pressured by his constant sexual hovering, and was rarely interested. Because Henry was a premature ejaculator, he felt like a bad lover, and believed this was the reason Hazel didn't want sex. The two of them were married for twelve years before their sexual difficulties even came up for discussion. Both were damaged by our culture's directive that we aren't to address sex openly.

Sal had an aversion to women's genitals, but also wanted sex at least once a day. He felt tremendous shame for his feelings, so he hid them from his wife. At the same time, he created a belief that there was something wrong with her vulva, to ease his shame by making it seem natural for him to feel this way. She picked up on his aversion and believed that his feelings were appropriate, without ever talking about it. She could understand that her vulva was repulsive to him. As a result, she encouraged having sex in the dark with no oral or manual stimulation of her genitals. She didn't have orgasms with intercourse alone, but this seemed like a small price to pay in order to meet his sexual needs, and her need to be an adequate sex partner. This shameful experience prevented her from wanting to engage in sex. She did so anyway until she was able to talk with a therapist.

For Fred, sex was too much work. He believed he was responsible for his wife's orgasm, and that he must orchestrate sex to a perfect conclusion. He had to make sure he didn't "accidentally" have an orgasm because then he lost interest in continuing, leaving her frustrated and angry. He preferred to avoid sex so he could avoid introducing a painfully difficult interaction. His wife was usually comfortable avoiding it too, but occasionally she wondered if he was attracted to her. She thought about losing weight, working out to make her body more attractive, and buying sexy clothing. She didn't know her looks had nothing to do with his lack of interest.

SEXUAL SECRECY

The secret anguish of these people, and many more like them, is the product of centuries of secrecy about sexual matters, and the resulting shaming of sexuality. The overlay of shame prevents people from knowing what sexuality really is, how to discover it and how to talk openly about it. Sexual recovery is necessary to really solve the problem of sexual differences. Quick solutions offered by sex therapists in women's magazines and therapy offices may seem helpful for a while, but with a subject that is overlaid with shame and false conceptions, real solutions take time. To bring sex out into the open, we can examine our feelings and beliefs about it, stemming both from our culture and our individual histories. In Chapter 4, I will describe how we have sex and avoid the feeling of shame. In

Chapter 10, I will show how we can strip the dreadful feeling of badness from our experience of our sexuality, making way for a wholesome alternative.

SHAME

What is the feeling of shame? While it takes many forms, it includes the belief that we are defective and should be different from who and what we are. John Bradshaw popularized the concept of "toxic shame," implying the need to "detoxify" from shame as one detoxifies the body from heavy use of drugs or alcohol, or from illness. (See *Healing The Shame That Binds You*, John Bradshaw, Health Communications, 1988, if you are interested in a thorough presentation on recovery from shame.) Shame is triggered by the thought or the experience of our perceived shameful nature as it is observed by others. Shame is attached to nudity, sexual activity, elimination, failure (real and perceived), put downs (a form of shaming) and countless facets of life for which we were shamed while growing up.

Shame is a debilitating feeling because, without therapy or other deliberate intervention, there is nothing that can be done to eliminate it. Guilt, on the other hand, comes when we believe we have done something wrong. It can be reduced by changing behavior, confessing or finding out that we haven't violated anyone. (Unhealthy guilt can, of course, be debilitating too. Methods used to cope with it can interfere with a life of integrity.)

If one feels shame for being a sexual person, nothing short of giving up sexuality will remove it. Since we as a race cannot do that and survive, sexuality continues anyway. **The effect is that all of us feel shameful and learn how to live with it.**

My editor, a woman who has long been on her own journey of sexual recovery, expressed discomfort in reading the examples from my sex life in this book. The rules we live by clearly state that we aren't to know details of the sex lives of people we associate with, particularly if they are more than acquaintances but not intimate friends. She quickly saw that she was responding to the very cultural sanctions that have required books such as this to be written!

YOUR SHAME

Reading this book may bring up your own feelings of shame about sexuality. My friend—I will call him Cam—is recovering from sex addiction, and still acts out occasionally. He was delighted to find that I had written this book, and eagerly wanted to read an early draft. But as he read stories that reflected his own he found that his sexual shame came up. This short book took him several weeks to complete because his shameful feelings made him want to act out, or in some way minimize the unpleasant experience. Once he could tell me this, and let himself read at a pace that brought up shame in manageable amounts, the feeling actually decreased. His new lover, on the other hand, had no difficulty reading. The nature of the book didn't make him uncomfortable.

I would like to encourage you to do what Cam did. Read at a rate that is comfortable for you. When shame or other unpleasant feelings come up, let them come and breathe so they can flow through your body and out.

You may find yourself sexually aroused while reading. If you do, allow yourself to feel it. There is no need to feel shameful or embarrassed about it, although of course you might anyway. The arousal is information about your sexuality, and can be used as part of the learning I am describing here. Members of my therapy and support groups are surprised when I tell them it is OK to be aroused by other people's stories. If they try to inhibit those feelings, or criticize them, they will cut themselves off from their bodies and experience, and stop their learning. After a time, clients comfortably tell when they are aroused, and get to learn from it.

SHAMING FROM YOUR PARTNER

Those who feel adventuresome and want to explore different ways to be sexual feel shamed when their partner doesn't agree. Bill married a woman who didn't want to try "new" things. On their honeymoon he wanted her to wear a tight skirt and high heels, walk into the outdoor hotel hot tub and have sex. Not only did she not want to do this, she shamed him, calling him a pervert. Their honeymoon was a disaster. After a few more such tries, Bill pushed his sexuality underground and lost interest in sex with his wife. The shame was too painful. He turned to pornography and masturbation instead, and told her he would continue until she sought therapy so that she could be freer with him. When the two of them entered therapy, they discovered that neither of their beliefs about the other's sexuality was accurate, and opened themselves to a new look at sex that could be enjoyable to both.

Bill also reacted to Alice's lack of arousal. She enjoyed receiving oral sex, but her body and voice did not communicate this, and so he didn't know she was receiving any pleasure. He felt strange putting his mouth on her vulva and experiencing no response. Intercourse was painful for her (we later learned the emotional reasons for this), although she was willing to have it anyway, to be a "good lover." Bill felt like a rapist. He soon lost interest in having sex with Alice because it was unpleasant to do so only for his own arousal and orgasm. He shamed her, calling her a prude and telling her something was wrong with her. For two years, they both avoided sex, until he insisted that the marriage would be over if she didn't do something. In time he found out that he too could make changes to allow the two of them the freedom to discover their sexual compatibility.

TRADITIONAL SEX THERAPY CAN MAKE PROBLEMS WORSE

Most behavioral sex therapists focus on the person who wants less sex, working to help that person increase sexual interest. While their techniques can work to a degree, the assumption that the "problem" lies with the less interested person is harmful to that person and to the marriage. When a person doesn't want sex there are very good reasons for it. These reasons must be respected first, and the person given permission *to have no sex for as long as necessary*. Sex therapists who do not understand sex addiction frequently encourage the less interested partner to be the sex drug to the addict. They suggest being romantic, dressing in "sexy" clothing, even losing weight and exercising in order to be more sexually appealing. These changes do nothing to enhance intimacy, or remove shame from sex. They encourage only an addictive sexual response.

The pervasiveness of sex addiction is only now becoming recognized as a cultural phenomenon. The constant sexual provocation from television and all around us feeds our addictive sides, and implies that intense, forbidden, lustful sex is "normal." It is not. *Almost all sex presented on television and movies is not in the scope of the natural function of sex, which is to bond two people into a loving couple, to marry them and to enhance their spiritual natures.* Sex therapists accept our culture's views of sex as normal, and then help people have more of that kind of sex. Our culture's view of sex is not only not normal, it contains all of the unhealthiness that pervades sexuality. As long as we accept the cultural view, we will encourage people to continue in activities that harm their spirituality. This inhibits people from discovering that there is far more to sex than our jokes and stories and hidden understandings.

Behavioral sex therapy, stemming from the work of Masters and Johnson, includes suggestions that people learn how to create fantasies to arouse themselves before and during sex. Also suggested is the use of erotic materials on video and in books. These things may indeed create arousal, but they prevent intimacy. When a man notices that his wife's eyes glaze over when they are being sexual, he may be seeing the effects of their therapist's recommendation to create arousal with fantasy. He is abandoned by her, left alone with his own fantasies.

The prescribed use of "sexy" clothing, sex videos, erotic stories or any other form of "outside-in" sexual stimulation will prevent a couple from finding out that healthy sexual arousal evolves from inside the two of them—it will prevent them from discovering intimate sex. The message from such therapists, consistent with everything we learn in our culture, is that shameful activity is OK. This permission can help *reduce the feelings of shame* while engaged in sex, but it does nothing to help *remove shame*.

Sex therapy conferences are just beginning to invite presenters who specialize in sex addiction. My hope is that in time this will broaden their understanding of the role of sex as a drug. Meanwhile, many sex addicts and their mates go to therapy for help, and are given advice that encourages the addict to continue an addiction. Furthermore, the mate is encouraged to become a better drug to satisfy the addict. This is reflected in "better sex" articles in women's magazines. I hear tragic stories resulting from lack of knowledge about sexuality—knowledge that is only now making it out to the public and to mental health professionals.

HEALTHY SEXUAL ENERGY

In my Healthy Sexual Energy classes I have seen many incredulous faces when I announce that healthy sexuality can only be possible if we say "no" to sex when we don't want it. Every time we say "yes" when it isn't in our very best interest, we re-violate ourselves. When I go on to talk about how sex therapists promote more sex as good sex, and teach arousal methods that violate us spiritually, I get two strong responses. One is relief and joy from those who felt constrained to obey the therapist. The second is anger and defensiveness from the addicted partner who wants his or her mate to cooperate by having more sex, not less.

My next book, *America's Sexual Crisis* (available in 1994), will describe some of the damage caused by traditional sex therapy.

Alecia and Paul went to many therapists over fifteen of their thirty-five years of marriage, trying to find out what they could do to have sex. Paul hadn't been able to ejaculate in his wife's vagina on the few occasions when he had been able to penetrate. Ten years into their marriage she had an affair in order to find out what sex was like.

When respected sex therapists questioned them about their sex life, they learned that Paul had had affairs. He had not only had intercourse, but had orgasms in vaginas! The therapists did not address sex addiction because fifteen years ago it wasn't generally understood. Instead, they placed the focus on what

Alecia could do so that Paul would be aroused by her in the same way he had been aroused by his lovers. She was taught to fantasize sexual scenes so she would be aroused prior to beginning sex with him, because Paul "needed" his lover to want him passionately. They were also instructed to collect videos of sex that aroused them, to watch them together and then have sex. During this time, Paul became able to stimulate his wife sexually, and both reported that their sex life had vastly improved. But Alecia continued to know that something was wrong with what they were doing. A friend gave her my first book, *Reclaiming Healthy Sexual Energy* (Health Communications, 1991), and she made an appointment to see me.

For the first time Alecia could see that she had been right about her beliefs that sex is supposed to be a loving act, not merely "getting off." The two of them embarked on a course of sexual exploration that opened their eyes. When Paul was able to give up his sex addiction, he soon found the use of pornography offensive. He felt deprived of the opportunity to truly be with his wife. For the first time in his fifty years, he discovered tender sexuality, truly making love with his mate. Alecia felt blessed by his change, although it was some time before he was able to have intercourse while being fully aware of her presence and his own. The details of "the act" lost importance as their loving emerged. They no longer had to settle for synthetic sex based on false stimulation. Eventually they were able to have intercourse and vaginal ejaculation, but these events were now in perspective. Without a goal, they offered freedom of choice to their bodies. The full spectrum of sexual activities were now available—but not required.

Alecia and Paul celebrated their thirtieth wedding anniversary with friends and family, repeating marriage vows that now make sense to both of them. The first time they publicly said they were marrying, both knew only the illusion of marriage.

Now they see each other's faults, know they want to be together and understand the role of sex in their lives. I am deeply touched to have had a part in their renewed relationship.

Chapter 2

The Addictive Use Of Sexual Energy Prevents Intimacy

Couples often argue over the frequency of sex because of the presence of sex addiction on the part of one or both partners. When one person is dependent on sex with a mate, the other will eventually feel pressured, obligated and resentful. In addition, he or she will feel unloved and used.

SEXUAL ADDICTION OF ONE PARTNER

Allen was afraid he couldn't make it through the day if he didn't have orgasms. He was easily stimulated by his fantasies and by women he found attractive. If he didn't end the arousal with an orgasm he would become intensely uncomfortably. He preferred to have sex with his wife because masturbation brought on additional feelings of shame. He had no understanding of this phenomenon, and so the only solution he could devise was asking his wife to help him with his "problem." They spent years having sex at least daily until Nancy read my book, *Reclaiming Healthy Sexual Energy*, and realized she was harming herself by using sex as a solution to sexual addiction. She brought her husband in to meet with me to discuss a possible course of action to address their sexual issues.

I could see the pain he went through each day as he was bombarded by sexual feelings. He focused on Nancy to save him from agony, and was quite disturbed by her decision to stop having sex until he could deal with his addiction. With no understanding of the parallel between the use of substances to change one's mood and the introduction of sexual arousal to do the same, he couldn't make sense of his sex life.

Emily described how Daniel acted as if he would die if she didn't have sex with him every day. The truth is, he really felt as if he would die. An addictive drug seems absolutely essential to the person who depends on it. Withdrawal from the sexual drug is extremely painful for those who are severely addicted.

Daniel's addiction was quite different from Allen's. Allen was addicted to sexual arousal, while Daniel was addicted to his wife. During his work day he thought of Emily, yearning for her touch. When he arrived home at night she was the first thing he wanted to see, hoping expectantly for a warm hug. When it wasn't forthcoming he was hurt, and his evening was less enjoyable.

When I suggested to Daniel that he was sexually addicted to his wife, he was shocked. He thought he loved her so much he would do anything to be with her, and that this was a great gift. He believed his wanting her was love because if she wanted him the same way he would feel loved.

Daniel worked on defining "sobriety." In contrast to sex addicts, who need to abstain from masturbation or prostitution to permit their recovery to begin, Daniel could see that sex with his wife was his equivalent to the alcoholic's drink. To him she was a drug. Sleeping in the same bed with her was painful because he couldn't think about very much besides initiating sex. He decided for a time that he would sleep separately in order to discover what it was like being with himself.

A turning point in his recovery came when he realized that he was angry about his role in his marriage as a "good boy," and that his fifteen-year infatuation with his wife prevented him from experiencing the anger. He decided not to be a good boy any longer, refused to listen to his wife talk about things that didn't interest him and took stands on issues he found important. As he both expressed his anger and changed the causes of it, he was able to let go of his forced positive regard for her. For the first time since his marriage at age twenty, he was able to ask himself what he really wanted sexually. He soon saw that he didn't want one-sided sexual relating. If Emily didn't really want to be sexual, he didn't either. He could see how painful it had been for him all those years to pursue someone who didn't want him. The drug status of sex made it seem worthwhile to beg her and try to get her to agree out of obligation. Now, as he respected himself, he could see how unhealthy this was for him.

Daniel also turned down sex when Emily initiated it, another first in their marriage. When she suggested sex, he checked to see if it felt obligatory on her part, or if she were trying to take care of him rather than expressing real interest in intimacy. He was ecstatic the first time he checked, saw that it didn't feel right, and said "no."

Kenneth was a sex addict, too, but his wife wasn't his drug. He went into sexual trances while searching fruitlessly for prostitutes, and then bought pornography and masturbated for many hours. Occasionally he went to a topless club and showed off his erect penis to a dancer, which brought him an addictive high.

He had difficulty feeling aroused during sex with his wife because of the time he spent rubbing his penis when masturbating. His penis had become insensitive to ordinary stimulation, and was often sore from the force of his touch. This caused intercourse to be an insufficient stimulus to maintain his erection unless he used intense fantasy. While he desperately wanted his wife to want him sexually, in fact, he had difficulty when she did.

Kathryn was confused by Kenneth's seemingly contradictory behaviors. She felt constantly pursued by him sexually, yet his body seemed to indicate that he wasn't interested. She knew he was a sex addict, but he hadn't been able to explain that his handling of his penis left him unable to respond to normal sex.

It is impossible for people who are sexually addicted, or those who are partners of sex addicts, to experience the kind of sexuality that emerges from inside of both people. The addiction, and the response to the addiction, becomes the focus of sexuality, preventing a knowing of the natural need for sex to bond and re-bond two people into a couple.

Jim had addictive sex with some men, and a physically affectionate relating with others. He deeply appreciated the cuddling he had with men who were close friends, and occasionally felt he was bonding into a mated state. But it was impossible for him to feel passionately sexual with a man he shared with intimately. The expression of sexual energy was only possible when in addiction.

SEXUAL ADDICTION OF BOTH PARTNERS

Jean married Dick because he loved sex as much as she did. She had been single for several years, and after her children were grown, she decided it was time to find a partner that was suited to her interests. She and Dick seemed perfectly compatible because they both wanted sex to be the center of their marriage. They set aside two hours to make love every night, and awoke to sex every morning before getting ready for work. They wrote each other love notes, and left phone messages focused on their sexual relationship. It seemed to be a perfect match. Neither had found another person so passionate about sex.

Yet, it didn't last. Gradually Jean found that she was so sexually satiated she no longer became interested. The morning sex, and even the noon sex on their days home, was tolerable because it only lasted a short time. But every evening Dick wanted to spend several hours preparing for sex and then engaging in it. He wanted her to dress up in "sexy" clothing and act out scenarios he had created in fantasy during the day. As time went on, she couldn't get aroused. She was astonished, because he seemed to be everything she'd dreamed of. Jean found out that it isn't possible to have addictive sex year after year, and continue to find it meaningful and fulfilling. As with drug addiction, it takes more of the drug or new drugs to continue to feed the addiction. *As Jean was required to be more and more of a drug to Dick, he was no longer able to be hers.*

A similar experience is described by Richard Rhodes in his autobiographical book, *Making Love* (Simon and Schuster, 1992). Rhodes describes his drugged joy when his new lover—Rhodes calls her G____was capable of seven or eight orgasms each time they had sex. Rhodes' drug, in real life or pornography, is women having orgasms, and so G____was the ultimate drug. In the beginning she liked his attention, having for the first time a man who seemed interested in her sexual satisfaction. But eventually she knew that it wasn't her he was interested in, but what she could do that stimulated him. In time their sex faltered, and he became frightened. Finally, she was able to tell him that she didn't want to have so many orgasms. She no longer liked his focus on how her body responded to his attention. She wanted to decide how many orgasms she would have. He asked her how many she thought that would be. She replied "one or two."

Rhodes' response to her declaration was classic for addicts whose drugs are taken away. He went crazy. He felt as if he were going to die. He believed the relationship was over, that he might as well pack up and leave. He stormed around the house for days, tormented, as intensely distressed as he must have been as a child when abandoned for life by his mother. His despair pours out on the page even though he wrote it years after the actual experience. Finally he came to terms with it, and was able to accept that their love making would no longer provide a major fix.

He doesn't describe G___'s feelings, but I know she must have prepared herself emotionally for her announcement, knowing that his reaction would be intense, and that he might leave her. But *being a drug isn't a suitable way to live*, and so eventually she had to do something. (Sex addicts may want to avoid reading this book because Rhodes' graphic descriptions of addictive sex could set off a trance state. For others it may be interesting to read an account of the pain and isolation of unrecognized sex addiction.)

Addiction to a partner can be more subtle than these examples. Henry was generally addicted to his wife, Hazel, although he didn't nag her for sex. Instead, his desire hung in the air, permeating their lives. Hazel was able to say "no," but she also believed she had to meet her marital requirement at least once a week. When a week had passed, she felt guilty, and then "took care of his needs." Her role in the addiction was providing the drug for him, whether or not he had asked for it, until she was able to understand that she was perpetuating the addiction. She had no alternative until she was able to decide to have no sex until it felt intimate.

THE SEXUAL ADDICT'S PARTNER

Looking at the relationship of Maggie and Richard, he seemed to be the addict and she his drug. He wanted to have sex when he felt lonely or rejected, reaching for her breast to relieve his bad feelings and replacing them with comfort and safety. If he could stimulate her sexually he felt reassured and loved.

Maggie grew to hate his touch when he felt like that, and the two rarely had sex. She felt fine about the idea of giving up sex forever because she was repulsed by his attempts to meet his infantile needs through her body.

But Maggie was the one who reacted, when the couples' group they attended suggested a sexual moratorium. The idea was for them to find out what would happen if they removed their sexual struggle from the relationship. She was terrified that if she weren't giving him sex he would leave her for another woman, or at the very least have an affair. As Richard identified the exact nature of his drug, and stopped using it, Maggie's terror increased. She began offering him more of his drug to reassure herself that he wouldn't abandon her. One morning she left him a love note, which he re-read throughout the day, each time receiving another "hit." By the end of the day he was afraid to go home and find out that she no longer felt the feelings she'd expressed in her note. This living in the future and the past showed him he had used the note as a drug.

Maggie spent several weeks in terror as he rejected each form of his drug. She wanted sex desperately to reassure herself that she had the power to hold his attention and to prevent him from leaving her for someone else. She was addicted to his desire for sex with her. Both Maggie and Richard were using sex for reasons that have nothing to do with intimate, bonding arousal. Their addictions prevented them from watching sex emerge from the inside out.

Addictive use of sexual energy is a major obstacle to the discovery of healthy sexual coupling, and one you might like to investigate further. The subject of sex addiction is well covered in four books listed under Sex Addiction in the Suggested Reading at the back of the book. If this might be an issue for you or your mate, I suggest you take a look at each book and read the one that seems most suitable. The information could help as you pursue the suggestions offered in later chapters.

Chapter 3

When Sexuality Becomes Cross-Wired

Another major reason couples have sexual difficulties is the presence of sexual "preferences" that interfere with loving sex with a mate. For example, Leslie's husband, Jeff, preferred masturbation with pornography over having sex with his wife. While his choice of pornography was to view heterosexual scenes of intercourse and oral sex, he couldn't translate these to his marriage. He was frightened of sex with a partner.

As Jeff was growing up, his body was violated by parents who spanked, tickled and poked at times he couldn't predict. He formed an emotional shell to shield himself from further violation. That allowed him to keep from experiencing their intrusions as violating. As a result, he associated his wife's touch with his parents', and the last thing he wanted then was the physical vulnerability of sexual arousal. He was forced to limit his sex life to solitary activity, which excluded his wife.

At the time I knew them, Jeff was unable to take on the task of remembering his childhood events with the attendant feelings. He couldn't release the past because he was too uncomfortable with the emotions, and because he had created a life of meaning in his work with computers. A brilliant thinker, he was

27

valued by his company for his creative work and his willingness to put his company before everything else. As long as he could masturbate occasionally with pornography, he was content with his life. He didn't have the motivation to take on the very hard work that accompanies retrieving feelings from childhood abuses.

His wife complained about the lack of sex, but she knew that if he were more interested, she would find herself less so. She'd also had a childhood in which her body hadn't been respected, and so it felt safe to have a husband who didn't want to touch her. At the same time, she felt hurt and less loved, which translated into the feeling of wanting sex.

ALL OF US ARE SEXUALLY CROSS-WIRED

All of us have our sexuality cross-wired in some fashion that prevents us from knowing healthy sexual energy. None of us managed to grow up without some shaming of our sexuality, and most of us ended up with a great deal. Shame is embedded into sexuality and sexual activity. The feeling of shame is one example of an emotion that becomes attached to sex that doesn't belong there. In fact, anything other than loving, bonding, joyful, intimacy-creating feelings are the result of overlays placed there by family and culture as we were growing up. It is possible to remove these overlays and to retrieve the healthy impulses we were born with. This is one of the goals of joining together with your mate to examine everything that comes up for you as you explore being sexual. (Chapter 3 in my book, *Reclaiming Healthy Sexual Energy*, offers more detailed information about how our culture shames us)

We are born into a culture that distorts our sexuality right from the beginning of life. Our bodies are shamed when evidence of sexuality emerges, as when boys have erections or girls touch their clitoris. By the time children reach the age of three or four, when sexual exploration and delight with sexuality emerge, most know they are not to reveal that they enjoy their genitals. I have heard the stories of the man whose father told him he would cut off his penis if he let it poke out over his pajamas, and the woman whose mother told her she was evil for showing her little brother that it felt good to rub their genitals against a chair. The vast majority of us grew up in families that didn't talk about sex, and by withholding this information, silently passed on the belief that sexuality is shameful. Silence, accompanied by laughter and whispers when talking to other adults, communicates as effectively as saying the words, "Shame on you."

Many damaging rules are imposed on sexuality, and are well understood by the time a young person reaches puberty, even though few were communicated with words. One rule is that we mustn't talk about sex in an open way. In spite of the multitude of articles in magazines and newspapers suggesting the importance of talking, no one enters my office with experience in really doing so.

Other rules are that we must service each other's sexual needs, that we must have sex if we are married or in a relationship and that it is OK if our partner has sex elsewhere if we aren't providing it. Prostitution and pornography are frowned on, yet billions of dollars are spent each year on sexual services. Sex therapists are now saying publicly that some kinds of pornography are useful.

Children are not allowed to develop their sexuality in natural ways. Instead, they are shamed, their physical and sexual boundaries are crossed, some are touched sexually and all are prohibited from a genuine sexual unfolding. With this background, all of us have had negative experiences that became associated with sexuality. We can remove these negative associations, but to do so we must talk and have the feelings that naturally accompany them, such as fear, humiliation, sadness or betrayal. Because our culture prohibits most discussion of sexual matters, and also discourages the full expression of emotion, the feelings from our early negative experiences get wired up to sexual activity, and to our choice of sexual partners. We play out our past experiences until we can bring them to consciousness and release them, thereby creating the opportunity to reclaim healthy sexuality. Chapter 9 details how the relationship can be the "container" for this kind of healing.

The media present examples of the connection between childhood experience and adult behavior. It is generally known that people who are sexual with children were probably sexually abused by an adult in their own childhood. It is also publicly understood that people who are abusive to their partners and children were abused in similar ways when they were children, and that people who tolerate abuse grew up with it. We *replicate those things that were unavoidable in childhood when we have no place to express the feelings that would have been appropriate.*

These connections occur most easily with sexuality because of the pervasive prohibition against acknowledging that it exists in children. We get stuck with the influence of both childhood experiences and cultural values in this area more easily than any other.

The term "cross-wiring" reflects the incorrect associations between sexuality and anything else that is not an inherent part of being sexual. For example, a rapist who must angrily take sex in order to be aroused is clearly not in touch with healthy sexual energy. He or she had experiences earlier in life which included cruel physical violation of boundaries that left sex attached to violence.

A second example is the need for pain in order to achieve orgasm. Known as sexual masochism, this form of cross-wiring can occur when children live with parents who are cruelly restrictive, and who humiliated them for their own cross-wired pleasure. Such children may grow up to be controlling and humiliating in their sexual or non-sexual life—duplicating what the parents did. Or they may, as adults, resume the child's role as victim of control and humiliation in various areas of life.

Activities that are wired up to sexual arousal are defined by the mental health profession as deviations from "normal." This includes sex with animals, urinating or defecating during sex, inflicting or receiving pain, the need to be punished or punish oneself, receiving enemas for arousal, focusing on objects or body parts (such as foot fetishes), the need to observe sexual scenes from a distance (voyeurism), the need to have one's genitals or sexuality observed (exhibitionism) and multiple hidden affairs when married. In addition, preference for mas- turbation over sex with a partner, the need for outside stimula- tion—such as pornography or fantasy—in a way that limits intimate sex and sexually addictive activities, are among issues that people bring to therapy. Some people manage to incorpo- rate their cross-wiring into their sex lives. For example, a couple may be drawn together because they share an interest in the same sexual fantasies, or someone who responds only to athletic bodies may mate with another who does too, and force each other to keep in shape. Most people who make it to my office, however, feel cursed by their cross-wiring and are aware that it prohibits intimacy with a mate.

With confusion in our culture over the subject of sex, it has been difficult for the mental health profession to decide what is normal and what is not. The definition of perversion has changed over the decades. In the past, homosexuality was considered "perverted," and a subject to address in therapy, even though the "cure" rate was low. After research on the subject, and pressure from homosexual mental health professionals and organizations, this is no longer routinely the case. But it's been difficult to know where to draw the line, and it changes according to what our culture accepts. We have gone from believing that the only healthy sex is heterosexual intercourse between married people, with the man on top, to accepting any activities between consenting adults. Such *assessments are based on the prevailing belief about right and wrong, rather than on the underlying truth about sexuality.*

The truth is that any cross-wiring, socially acceptable or not, will prevent intimate sex. Those who can only be sexual with thin people are greatly limited in their choice of a partner. If a thin partner gains weight, the partner who is cross-wired to thinness will no longer respond sexually. This form of cross-wiring is built into our culture and seen as normal. Women and men are encouraged to lose weight and exercise to make their bodies sexy. In fact, their sexuality is no different when thin or plump. It may feel different because outside-in self-esteem can drop when we don't measure up to our culture's ideals. Therapists often work with a person to increase their "attractiveness" (as defined by our culture's values) so they can feel better about themselves.

Some people's cross-wiring creates an attraction to certain kinds of facial expressions. They need to see the expressions in order to stimulate sexual interest; which can include loving, frightened, angry, friendly and withholding, as well as seductive. A glance at ads in magazines or television reveals the power of these various expressions in drawing the attention of viewers.

Sexual activities can be cross-wired too. If oral sex is necessary for arousal, then the person is prevented from finding out what his or her body would like to do. Specific ordering of activities is not part of unfolding discovery of behaviors that are right at the time.

If two people cannot be intimate when sexual, they will eventually experience differences in their desire for sex and in their feelings about each other.

NEW CRITERIA FOR "UNHEALTHY" SEX

The concept of cross-wiring allows us to disregard the question of what is moral and acceptable and turn, instead, to a different set of criteria to decide if something is "wrong."

These criteria might include the following:

1. Does my cross-wiring interfere with finding and maintaining a loving, intimate relationship?

2. Is my sexual focus more on how to achieve arousal and orgasm than on experiencing my partner more completely, and being seen for who I am?

3. Does my cross-wiring dictate my sexual choices? That is, partners, activities, feelings, sexual frequency, etc.

4. Does my cross-wiring bring feelings of shame, either from within me, or from the thought of others knowing?

5. Does my cross-wiring prevent me from using sex as a loving expression toward myself or another?

6. Does my cross-wiring inhibit the use of sexual energy to bond me into a monogamous, committed relationship?

SHAME IS AN OBSTACLE TO FINDING HEALTHY SEXUAL ENERGY

Feelings of shame for any sexual activity between consenting adults are misplaced, and an additional example of cross-wiring. We were given shameful associations that remained bound up to our sexuality. Events out of our control placed them there, and we are stuck with that until we have an avenue for change. We are not bad people for wanting to have sex with animals or for finding bondage arousing or for responding sexually to movie rape scenes.

Sexual fantasies of any kind are not indicators that something is morally wrong. Fantasies are merely indicators of what got wired up during an earlier time of life, and thus provide valuable information. (Guilt is appropriate when another person is being harmed, especially children or those who are coerced into sex. Toxic shame is never useful to a person who wishes to change sexual wiring.)

Once we are able to take a shame-free, curious look at our sexuality, then we can begin to examine how our connections were made. As I began my own curious exploration, I could see just how pervasive cross-wiring of sexual energy is. Some of your own cross-wiring may seem of no consequence, while some may greatly affect your sexual relating with your partner.

Below are categories of cross-wired behaviors and examples of each. Within these categories the particular behaviors can be high or low on the scale of social acceptability. For example, a man who is aroused by using overtly sexual, "dirty" language is not acceptable if he does this with strangers on the street, but is tolerated and even encouraged when he does so with a partner who is sexually responsive to such behavior.

Categories of Sexually Cross-Wired Behavior

1. **Visual stimuli**

   hair color
   "sexy" clothing
   a certain body weight and shape and other physical
     qualities
   body positioning and movement
   nipple placement on breast

2. **Specific sexual activities essential for arousal**

   oral sex
   anal sex
   use of certain body positions and movements, etc.

3. **Non-sexual activities essential for arousal or orgasm**

   spanking or being spanked
   being tickled
   bondage
   talking "dirty"
   creating genital pain
   biting, pinching, scratching
   urinating or defecating
   use of fetish objects
   wearing of certain clothing

4. **Erotic stimuli in the environment**

   a "sexy" person walking down the street
   someone undressing
   sound of a zipper
   scent of perfume, aftershave or cologne

sex talk

pictures or movies of sexual scenes

5. Feelings that produce arousal

feeling aroused by a lover walking away

wondering if arousal will occur (i.e., through massage)

wanting to be seduced, or to seduce

feeling special and important

feeling sexy to your partner

feeling admired, physically or otherwise

feeling loved

6. Clothing

tight clothing that shows off the body to others,
  bringing arousal

men wearing women's clothing & vice versa

feeling well dressed

clothing sold in sex stores and catalogues,
  designed to arouse

7. Alteration of yourself to seem "sexy"

body positioning

strutting

smiling

making sexual sounds

touching one's body suggestively

flirting

8. Romance

needing to be charmed, swept off her/his feet, made
  to feel special

needing to feel like a real man, a stud, with above
  average genitals, and ability to perform.

taking care of and being taken care of (financially,

emotionally, physically, etc.)

quickly believing that this is *the* relationship, and is permanent

reading romance novels frequently

9. **Discussing sex as wicked, forbidden, naughty, dirty**

telling "dirty" jokes

approaching potential partner with overtly sexual come-ons

talking "dirty"

10. **Your sexual role**

the "other woman" or "other man" in triangles

the "bad girl"—having sex with almost anyone

"super stud"—getting any girl

prude

the "good girl"

the gentleman, or good guy

knight in shining armor

shy, bashful, "come after me" or "I'm afraid of you."

11. **Fear of sex**

avoidance of sexual activity

lack of arousal when it would be appropriate

staying out of relationships

having impersonal sex to avoid fear brought on by awareness of partner

preferring masturbation to sex

time to leave or go to sleep after orgasm

12. **Fear of relationships**

13. **Preference for sex without a partner**

fantasies of sex and sexual relationships are preferred for arousal pornography replaces sex with a real person

voyeurism—looking at strangers

indirect sexual interaction—telling sexual jokes, mentioning the night to come at a wedding, double entendres in conversation, flirting

14. New partners necessary for arousal

15. Having sex because you can't say "no"

because you're in a relationship

because you did it once before with that person

because you can't turn it down

because there seems to be no relationship without it

because he/she wanted you

16. Sexual activity has particular meaning

you are loved

you are a loving person

you are valued

you are wanted

you are beautiful/handsome

life has meaning

you are safe

17. Sexual activity has a function

as tranquilizer or sleeping pill or other mood altering "drug"

as something to do

to create closeness when it doesn't occur in other ways

to reduce stress

18. Flirting when not looking for a relationship

to feel powerful over the one who responds

to feel powerful over the mate of the one who
  responds
to bring on a socially acceptable sexual charge
to feel attractive

19. **Responding with sexual energy involuntarily**

to television and magazine ads designed to trigger
  sexual energy
to flirtations with people who are not available, or
  when you are not available
to the walk, dress, facial expression, etc., of those
  who exude sexual energy (often seen as charismatic)

20. **Socially unacceptable partners**

children
post-pubescent teens
siblings
parents
animals
people of vastly differing ages

Cross-wiring is pervasive in our culture, as can be seen in many of the examples above. *The automatic sexual "hits" we get while watching television, and even walking down the street, are accepted as natural. They are not.* Rather, they are examples of cross-wiring that almost everyone experiences. They interfere with you and your mate finding out what is possible sexually. In *Reclaiming Healthy Sexual Energy*, I describe the process by which we become cross-wired, and the healing process that will release us from it.

Chapter 4

More Reasons Why Couples Differ

We can discover the healthy functions of sex when we are in touch with our sexual selves, and with the sexual self of our mate. We can easily make decisions about when and how to have sex. A major obstacle to this kind of awareness is the enormous shame that our culture and our families have laid onto sex. Examining this overlay can provide information about how to relinquish it.

THE SHAME COMPARTMENT

Sexuality was considered a shameful subject during childhood and we've learned not to talk about it. In addition, we had countless shameful experiences and saw the shame of others when they revealed sexual information. The laughter at jokes about sex further reinforced the shameful nature of sexuality. With this background, how is it possible to fall in love, get married, and immediately interact with our mate from a place of sexual health? It isn't. *Instead, we have to figure out ways to incorporate shame into sex so that we don't feel it.*

We do this by accepting ourselves as shameful during the time we engage sexually. This allows us not to feel the shame. (You can demonstrate this temporary identification with shame by thinking about what happens if your mother calls during sex, or if she knocks on the door or, worse, walks in on you. You feel embarrassment, a form of shame. The stimulus of her presence brings you back into the world and alerts you to the rest of your feelings about sex.)

Putting ourselves into the shame compartment requires taking certain steps. *We move out of where we experience shame about sex and into a place where doing something shameful feels OK.* Those who feel sexual all the time live in the shame compartment, and so they don't have to do anything in particular to get there. For example, the stereotype of a male construction worker is a man who is always searching for sexual stimuli, and who is always feeling sexual. As a result, he will call out sexually to attractive women, pin up "sexy" pictures and lace his conversation with jokes and sexual innuendo. By incorporating sexual shame into his very being, he can have his sexuality and avoid the feeling of shame at the same time. Those who find him disgusting are outside the shame compartment. Their shame is available for them to feel. But these same people will go to sex-laced comedy shows or soft porn movies in order to enter their shame compartment, and will also find jokes and innuendos entertaining. Most of us choose to move in and out, and all of us have seen people who stay in. They are disturbing to us because they represent an exaggeration of our own maneuvers to be sexual people.

My own sexual healing gave me a personal understanding of the shame compartment. As I removed shame from sex, I no longer had to enter a separate reality to be sexual. The decision to be sexual became no big thing—just another way to be me.

When I had to get into my shame compartment, it took being newly in love or an effort of shifting consciousness. Then when sex was over, I again felt shame unless I did something to avoid it, such as erasing it from my mind. In some way I separated it from my usual view of myself, seeing sex as something in a different category, one I visit from time to time.

I can see the remaining evidence of the shame compartment when my husband Rex and I are kissing in our office and someone walks in. I immediately pull away from him as if we have been caught doing something wrong!

We are encouraged to separate sex from life by society as well as by our individual shame. Think about what it would be like if your friends and co-workers talked about their evenings or weekends and included sex as one of the things they were going to do, or had done. For example, you're at your desk at work and you say, "Hey, Judy, what are you and Bill doing Saturday night?" Judy answers, "Oh the usual. We'll probably go bowling, have pepperoni pizza and then have oral sex on his couch in front of the TV."

In contrast, your acquaintences only talk about sex if they are in the shame compartment—for example, men are allowed to show off and brag about the woman they picked up the night before. But once they fall in love with a woman they "respect," they can't talk about her in that manner because they believe it shames her. Sex has to be isolated to prevent it from being experienced shamefully.

During the early period of bonding into a couple, when sex is vitally important to creating families, shame is easier to overcome. Sex has a spiritual purpose that pushes the shame away for a time. But once the bonding is complete, then various maneuvers become necessary in order to keep feelings of shame from surfacing. If you stay in the present, which is necessary to experience intimacy, then shame will surface. (This becomes a valuable tool to strip shame from sex because shame has to be felt before it can be removed.)

If you and your partner are using habitual methods of getting into the shame compartment to have sex, and are consequently out of touch with your real interest in sex—yours and your partner's—you cannot know how much sex either of you wants. Shame also prevents you from knowing the purpose of sex in your lives, and how to use sex to bond and re-bond. And your bodies can't communicate with each other (leaving intellect out of it) and they can't make the decisions about what to do and when. *Shame, and what we have to do to avoid it, prevents loving sex.*

My own experience of the shame compartment showed up when I looked at pornographic magazines with my husband, Rex, as part of his sexual healing. Over the course of several years he made sculptures and paintings that told the story of his childhood and resulting cross-wiring. During this time, he saw that he needed to go to an "adult" bookstore and find pictures that brought up his cross-wired shame so that he could make drawings of similar scenes. In the process, he worked through his shame and successfully eliminated almost all of his cross-wiring. Childhood events and relationships that had been damaging became evident.

Early in my first marriage, I read *Playboy* magazine in order to become aroused so that I could meet my sexual obligations. I felt absolutely no shame for this behavior, and could actually tell people I trusted. My husband, who had bought the magazines, knew about it. At that time I thought that I had no shame about what I was doing—I didn't understand the shame compartment, and how it operates to allow me not to feel shame that is actually present. I discovered it when Rex invited me to go to the bookstore to buy the magazines.

I felt so much shame over the idea of walking into the store and seeing other customers in sexual trances searching for their fixes, that I had to say no. He went by himself anyway, and brought five magazines home to show me. As we sat on our living room couch leafing through the pages, my shame flew up. But over the hour or so that we looked at pictures, acknowledging which ones were arousing and which were not, my shame dropped. I could see that these were just pictures of people doing sexual things, and there was no reason for me to feel shame. In fact, it was necessary to go back to all my cross-wired stimuli, let them arouse me and remain conscious. The shame that emerged while in this healing process dropped away, and has been replaced by the inability to be aroused by cross-wiring. As we heal from it we can become free from outside-in arousal.

As these pictures were pinned up in Rex's art studio, and transformed with paint and canvas into his versions, my shame stayed down. When friends came to visit, varying amounts of shame re-emerged, allowing me to eliminate one more layer. By staying out of the shame compartment, and feeling the shame, I was able to release large portions of it.

Among the ways we prevent ourselves from feeling shame are the following:

1. The use of sexual fantasy. During sex many people think about having sex with someone else, or somewhere else, or doing something else. This prevents knowing what is going on in the present. If we define intimacy as knowing the other and being known by them, then fantasy prevents that. Instead, the one who fantasizes is creating a new partner or a new activity or a new place. Illusions replace reality.

While having sex, Jeffrey always imagined his wife was an older woman who sought to take care of him sexually. This fantasy allowed him to become aroused while his wife's body and manner did not. Fantasizing allowed him to avoid his issues. It also prevented him from finding out that sexual abuse by an aunt when he was pre-pubescent had affected his understanding of sex. Once he was able to talk about his experiences with his aunt, and have the feelings that weren't permitted at the time, he was able to see who it was he was really having sex with. The fantasy became unnecessary.

2. The use of pornography and erotica. When "ordinary" sex with a partner doesn't work, people may rely on erotic materials. These sexually arousing stimuli feed into a person's cross-wiring; that is, the propensity to link sex to things that aren't sexual, but which result in intensely sexual feelings. The feelings induced by erotic materials are so intense that they dispel the shame that would come up during "ordinary sex." Once shame is dispelled from sexuality, then arousal becomes free and easy, and erotica has no appeal. We no longer need a strong sexual jolt to get things going sufficiently to propel us into the shame compartment.

I saw the effects of being on the outside of the shame compartment when I took a large drawing of penises to my men's therapy group, and pinned it up on the wall. Every one of the men in the group had used pornography to become aroused, and several had actively collected magazines and videos to feed their addiction. Their shame surfaced only when they were finished masturbating. Yet when I introduced a picture of penises that could never be considered pornographic, a number of shame reactions emerged. Some were overtly feeling discomfort and turning red. Others were angry, criticizing the presence of the picture in the room. Still others could not see clearly that the drawing actually portrayed erect penises. One man did not see that white drops were coming out from the ends of them. His most intense cross-wiring, and shaming, was associated with ejaculation.

During an hour of discussion, the feelings diminished, and the picture became merely a colorful addition to the office. As shame subsided, intense attention to the stimulus was no longer evoked. The men could see this scene without shame, and were no longer defensive or otherwise uncomfortable.

3. Sexual arousal. Becoming aroused dampens our sexual shame. This is the reason sexual arousal is a major addiction—it is powerful enough to let us eliminate shame and other unpleasant feelings. Many people use sexual arousal to meet their sexual "requirements" to be a "man" or a "woman" or a person "in a relationship." This results in people thinking about sex during the day, becoming aroused and then initiating sex when it becomes possible. I believe this accounts for the myth that men become aroused faster than women. Men are expected to be always ready for sex, and they may look and think lustfully to keep themselves arousable. When sex becomes possible, their physiology is already engaged prior to direct stimulation. Women who prepare themselves in the same way (which our culture does not require) also find that arousal occurs rapidly when they are stimulated.

Erik was unable to respond to his wife's sexual overtures, and felt inadequate when he didn't get an erection immediately. His general feelings of sexual shame, and his shame over his inability to "perform," made him feel different from other men. His solution, however, allowed him to fit right in with the American male stereotype. He searched for sexual stimuli on billboards, in store windows and from watching women walk down the street to keep him in a constant state of mild arousal.

TV ads helped in the evening before going to bed. His arousal allowed him to act in ways he believed were necessary. He didn't face up to the effects of his shame until he became depressed over the loss of his job, and was unable to use familiar methods of getting into the shame compartment. His fear, well beyond that to be expected from temporary loss of interest in sex, became so intense that he found it necessary to see a therapist.

4. Cross-wired stimulators. Cross-wiring that results in intensely driven sexual stimulation is a shame inhibitor. By calling on experiences from childhood that became linked up with sexual arousal, it is possible to bring on arousal and combat shame. Any activities from the list in Chapter 3 that bring a sexual jolt can be used. Again, this sexual jolt interferes with intimacy as well as preventing shame from emerging.

Tom insisted his wife wear rose perfume whenever they had sex. We discovered that his mother once wore that perfume when he had an erection in her presence.

In his book, *Making Love*, Richard Rhodes described his obsession with female orgasms. His current lover thought he was vitally interested in pleasing her, but later learned that when she didn't want to have more than one or two orgasms, he was devastated. When we focus on specific stimuli to arouse us, that interferes with our achieving intimacy with a partner. It also prevents shame from emerging.

5. Addictive use of sexual energy. Needing sex as a drug holds shame at bay because the need for the drug outweighs the power of the shame. If it didn't, sex addicts wouldn't act out. For example, when Kenneth's self-esteem was high, he had no interest in looking at female body parts. However, the constant experience of being in the shame compartment reduces self-esteem, and increases our need for the addiction to override the experience of shame. Sex addicts find that when they can become "sober" for a period of time, they feel better about themselves, and find it easier to stop the addiction.

6. Alcohol and other drugs. Mood-altering substances can artificially open a person to sexual arousal by reducing shame and fear and acting as an aphrodisiac, making it easier to get into the shame compartment. There are numerous ways by which we reduce or avoid shame. By stripping shame from sex, we can't feel the shame. And if we can't feel it, we can't remove it. *And if we can't remove shame, that keeps healthy, spiritual sexuality from emerging.*

PERFORMANCE PRESSURES

Men are required to be "good lovers," always ready for sex, and must make sure to met their partner's "needs." Men must like to give oral sex and be sensitive to their partner's feelings. Men are allowed no room to be bungling, clumsy and new at this hidden, secret activity. With this kind of pressure, how can a man learn about sex, about his mate and about his fears and shame? I am surprised men even want sex when it is so much work. But not to want it labels them as something other than men. They are doomed either way.

Women have to perform too. A woman must look right so the man gets aroused. She mustn't be too direct in initiating sex so she doesn't make him feel pressure to perform, and she has to be sensitive to his needs so he doesn't get turned off by her demands. She has to have (or fake) an orgasm so he feels like a good lover.

The requirement to perform is a huge obstacle to finding loving, unfolding sex. It is a disastrous form of cross-wiring that comes with living in this culture. *Sexual performance results in two people working together to create something that meets our society's definition of sex.* When this happens, natural, unfolding sex is impossible. Performance cannot be part of healthy sexuality. Instead, if each person identifies the performance pressure as it comes up, and experiences the feelings associated with it, he or she can gradually abandon this unhealthy approach to sex.

CHILDHOOD SEXUAL ABUSE

A major obstacle to natural sexual expression is the abuse of sexuality during childhood. Those who were the objects of overt sexual contact in childhood will always feel the effects on their adult sexuality. These effects can be cleaned away by allowing feelings to surface during sex with a trusted partner, knowing they are from the past, and discharging them. My own experience included body memories during sex and at other times, as well as expectations of abuse from my partners that had little to do with them. Over time I gave myself permission to put these feelings first, no longer seeing "the sex act" as primary. With repeated discharges of feelings, I have eradicated most of the cross-wiring that came from inappropriate sexual contact during my childhood.

Relationships that were not overtly sexual, but where sexual energy was part of the relating, will also have an impact on adult sexuality. For example, Trina's mother was a sex addict, and sexualized her relationship with Trina along with most other people in her life. She was angry with her husband for not providing enough sex to satisfy her, and rejected him in favor of Trina. In her marriage, Trina found herself acting out her mother's patterns. She rejected her husband sexually (even though he was a sex addict, and wanted her constantly) and focused her sexual attention on her daughter. Discovering the connection and working together with her husband to become conscious of her actions allowed Trina to have feelings from her past and so change the effects in the present.

The abuse of sexuality during childhood is a major reason people have sexual difficulties later. As our culture shifts, and the fact of child sexual abuse as a cultural phenomenon is believed, more and more of us can see the truth and make changes that will allow us full sexual expression. Therapy groups and Twelve Step groups for child sexual abuse survivors, as well as individual therapy, are vital to this recovery. The feelings are deep and intense, and the need for safe support is vital. If your sexual work reveals memory of such abuses, I encourage you to seek help. Working with your mate alone is not sufficient.

THE NEED TO SAY "NO" TO SEX

You cannot really say "yes" to sex if you cannot say "no." Our culture has jokes about how to communicate "no." Women are allowed to have headaches. Men are allowed to find their mates unattractive. If a women isn't sexually attractive, a man can attribute his lack of interest in sex to that, implying that if she only looked or acted differently, then he could get an erection and be able to perform. Countless women have gone on diets, bought sexy clothing and had breast implants to be good enough sex objects, when the solution really lies in men giving themselves permission to say "no" when they don't feel like being sexual. Men are set up by our culture's definition of "real men" to see lack of interest as the woman's fault.

When a man can say "no" to sex, he has an opportunity to find out about his feelings of obligation. He can discover his aversion to women's bodies, to sex and to shame and fear associated with sexual activity. He can also identify the cross-wiring he uses to overcome shame and fear so that he can be sexual anyway.

Barry was forty-one, and hadn't had a relationship longer than a year until he partnered with Tammy. Each time he found himself losing interest in sex with his lover, and then introduced his cross-wired interest into the sexual relating to override his lack of interest. Eventually this didn't work, and as he became more and more distant from his lovers for this and other reasons, he ended the relationships.

Tammy began working on her sexual healing about the time Barry was losing interest because the bonding phase had ended. She refused to position her body so that he would receive a cross-wired sexual jolt in order for him to be able to "make love" to her. She also refused to assume the facial expression that he found sexual. The relationship might have ended at this point if Barry hadn't decided he needed to enter therapy too. Armed with an understand of cross-wiring and addictive use of sexual energy, he was able to explore the reasons why he was repulsed by Tammy's body, and why his cross-wiring took the particular form it did. Only when he could refuse sex, for any reason at all, did he have the freedom to discover what was going on. He had the support of the men's group when he expressed his distaste for Tammy's—and every other lover's—body. Tammy dealt with her initial feelings of hurt and rejection and, once they were expressed, she could see that Barry was imprisoned by his past experiences. She could know they had nothing to do with her.

WE CAN'T RESPOND HEALTHILY TO A PARTNER'S CROSS-WIRING

Healthy sex unfolds naturally between two people. If one person is responding from a place of cross-wiring or addiction, then the partner cannot have healthy sex, either. This fact has confused many people who felt genuine love for their mate, wanted to be sexual, but found themselves resistive. This "problem" is brought to sex therapists, and treated as if it were, indeed, the problem. On the contrary, *it is always healthy to turn down sex any time that it doesn't emerge from inside out, from both people.*

SEX EXPRESSES ANGER AND CONTROL

It is a tragedy of our culture that anger and control are commonly cross-wired to sexuality. The result is that couples are often drawn together to satisfy these "needs," and then find it impossible to use sex lovingly.

If you find yourself sexually triggered by rape scenes, you are not the only one. You may think you are, because few people will admit to this reaction. But take a look at movies that use rape scenes to engage us sexually. The popular movie, *Thelma and Louise*, shows us shots of Geena Davis's pants being pulled off, revealing her underwear in a way that is obviously intended to be seen as sexual. This is confusing because the stated purpose of the scene is to show us how brutal the man is, and we are further invited to identify with the desire to kill him.

When I reacted to this scene with a sexual "hit," I immediately compartmentalized my response, holding it separate in my mind because I knew I "should" be feeling only rage at the man and a desire to protect Geena. When Susan Sarandon holds a gun on him and finally pulls the trigger, I am vindicated. Not only do I get to see this brutal man stopped from ever again violating a woman, I also get to have my own cross-wiring to rape eradicated—for the moment, at least.

It may be difficult for you to own your feelings of anger when asking your mate for sex. It may also be difficult to own your desire to be in control—particularly as she or he thwarts that control by saying no. *When one partner is expressing anger through sex, both people are violated.*

Henry asked for sex every night through his body language and sighs. When Hazel didn't indicate willingness, he felt betrayed and hurt. Yet during periods when Hazel was eager for sex to satisfy her own cross-wired arousal, Henry didn't respond. He lost his control when she was sexually active. His expression of anger was satisfied when she felt pressured and reluctantly agreed to sex once a week or so to satisfy her marital requirement. His anger at her was expressed at those times, and was also expressed when she didn't want sex but felt guilty and pressured. He was in control, even though it didn't look as if he got what he wanted.

Any time one or both partners are meeting "needs" that have nothing to do with sex, they will be confused about what sex really is. It cannot be clear to either person when and how to express sex. It is also likely that the one who is exhibiting anger and control will be the one who expresses an interest in more sex, and the person who is the object of these feelings the one who wants less.

You might recognize your own anger and control expressed through sex if you have the following experiences:

1. Anger when your partner says "no" to sex
2. Thoughts about what to do next to get her or him to agree
3. Resentment carried through hours or days
4. Thoughts about finding someone else to have sex with
5. Setting out to seduce a partner

6. Dressing, speaking or acting provocatively, whether with a mate or a stranger

7. Being seductive with another person in the presence of your mate

Any time anger or control is part of sex, it isn't possible to open yourself and allow sexual energy to flow gently and comfortably through you—a step which is necessary for finding the right sexual frequency and the useful activities.

DISLIKE OF PARTNER'S SEXUAL INTERESTS

Couples entering therapy often find out that one person doesn't want to have sex with the other because of the other's interest in a particular cross-wired form of sex. For example, if one partner wants to use pornography and the other objects then the latter will appear less interested in sex. *This healthy refusal to engage in cross-wired sex is often labeled a "problem" by therapists trained in traditional approaches to sex therapy.*

Lynn told me she felt like a prude when she didn't want to "experiment" with sexual activities her husband suggested. He knew he was a sex addict, but wasn't aware that many of his seemingly normal preferences were also not healthy. I affirmed for her that she was on the right track when she refused to have sex when James wasn't present with her. She had no interest in being seduced or romanced, or having sex in places that added the risk of being caught. After ten years of being told she was sexually inhibited, and being encouraged to read sex books to loosen up, she had her first confirmation that this was not at all the case. She very much enjoyed sex when her husband was present with her.

James was a victim of his history, and so he hadn't been able to appreciate that sex was possible without the extra stimulation of fear, lust and romance. He had been introduced to pornography as a boy of about five by his teenage uncle, and his feelings had become eroticized by it. His uncle showed him pictures of many kinds of unusual sex, while talking with sexual energy about how he would like to be involved. James doesn't remember being physically stimulated by his uncle, but he does remember feeling sexually stimulated by the talk and sexual body language. He grew to believe that this intense, avid sexual feeling his uncle expressed was normal, and that his own response was, as well. He grieved over the loss of this kind of camaraderie shared in secret, with shame intensifying the bond and the arousal. He believed his wife should join him as he had joined his uncle, so the two could have their intense, secret life. He was angry when she refused, trying to create guilt to pressure her into it, and initially felt chagrined when I supported her position. He was propelled into another piece of work on his incestuous past.

Couples are confused when some activities seem to work in the early period of their relationship, but then fall apart because one person can no longer handle that approach to sex. A woman came to see me after she experienced severe distress during a sexual encounter with a man she had been dating. I was in doctoral training in the late Seventies in a college counseling center, with no education that could allow me to help her. She and her lover had sex for many hours at a time, and engaged in sado-masochistic acts that in the beginning she had found highly stimulating. However, months into the relationship, after a night of simulated torture, restraint and rape, she broke into tears and sobbed out of control for several hours.

She made an appointment at the counseling center where she received no help from me. Sex therapy didn't address this, and at that time it wasn't generally understood that memories of sexual abuse could be elicited by current sexual situations. The very fact that she found such situations arousing indicates that she had been abused in cruel ways earlier in her life. I didn't know then that she was trying to tell her story by the sexual choices she made, and by the feelings that finally emerged.

Her lover didn't understand why she reacted as she did. His shame was triggered by her response because she had gotten out of the shame compartment, leaving him alone and seen. He was unable to stay in by himself. Because he believed he had no other choices for sexual expression, he ended the relationship, moving on to another woman who could meet his "needs." He had apparently learned years before that women would not continue to engage in sex in ways he found arousing, and so prepared himself by never committing to a relationship. I am guessing that he also couldn't have been married to a woman who would engage in simulated torture because when they were out of the shame compartment, leading a regular life, he would feel the shame of his sexual choices. He had led an isolated life, not knowing there was help for his cross-wiring.

PREFERENCE FOR MASTURBATION

Some people develop their own sex lives early, around puberty, and prefer solitary expression over sex with a mate. There are a number of reasons for this: fear of people, the belief that one isn't an acceptably sexual person, anger at partners that interfere with using sex lovingly and cross-wiring so intense that it only allows a person to become highly aroused when stimulating himself or herself. The result is that that person's partner, if there is one, is likely to be dissatisfied with the lack of sex. The partner's discovery of the solitary sex life usually leads to feelings of abandonment and rejection, particularly if pornography is used as stimulation.

William came to therapy because his wife objected to the lack of sex. They said he just didn't have any interest in his sexuality, and had been diagnosed as having "inhibited sexual desire." But when we met alone for a few times, and William believed that I would keep his confidence, he revealed that his sexual desire was present, but he preferred to masturbate rather than have sex with his wife or any other woman. Consistent with his sexual preference, William was a loner who preferred spending time with his computers over being with people.

WHEN ONE PARTNER PREFERS A DIFFERENT GENDER

Many homosexual people marry someone of the opposite sex with the hope that they can lead a normal-looking life and not have to face the difficulties that comes with belonging to an oppressed group. Difficulties arise if the gay partner isn't interested in having sex with his or her spouse.

Frances was drawn to Ryan because he didn't immediately come on to her sexually as her other boyfriends had. She had more room to be drawn to him, and to pursue him, too. He wasn't possessive as the others had been and so she felt she could tolerate being married to him because he wouldn't want to control her.

Ryan was a professional, and valued his career. Believing that he couldn't continue in his work if he was seen as gay, he asked Frances to marry him, and she was delighted. Meanwhile he maintained his interest in men, even though he was able to have sex to conceive children and to prevent her from knowing the truth.

In the early years of their marriage, he limited his homosexual life to masturbation with fantasy and pornography, but eventually decided to have sex with men. At first he had only casual sex with them, but eventually found himself in short-term relationships. Frances intuited the truth, but couldn't let herself find out for sure until they had been married for over thirty years and their children were grown. She caught him in the act. Frances felt as if the marriage were over, although she stayed with him. She couldn't imagine separating when they were almost sixty and had established a long-term lifestyle together.

Ryan's dishonesty about his sexual preferences prevented both of them from finding out how they really wanted to live, and created enormous, insoluble conflicts in their sex life. Alcohol was necessary for both of them to remain blind to the sexual struggles of so many years.

A woman I knew some time ago was trying to find out if she was a lesbian or heterosexual. After initially being sexual with men in her teen years, Barbara felt relieved to find that sex with women presented fewer difficulties, and identified herself as lesbian. She formed a relationship with a woman, and became part of the lesbian community. Still, after several years, she found herself attracted to a man and began to have sex with him. Her partner was devastated and felt betrayed, but then was able to make sense of the sexual difficulties the two had experienced. Her partner realized that she had received information about this, but hadn't let herself acknowledge it, preferring to accept Barbara's reassurances.

Some people have homosexual cross-wiring, but are drawn to, and fall in love with, people of the opposite sex. If the person acts on the cross-wired interest, sex addiction may be the motivation. If the attraction to the same sex is due only to cross-wiring, rather than a genuine desire for bonding, and isn't the fuel for addiction, then it's possible to choose not to act on it.

But as long as addiction is present, then the partner may act out the addiction by using the homosexual cross-wiring as the form the addiction takes. For example, Glenn truly loved his wife and often enjoyed their sexual relating. But he was also a sex addict. His acting out took the form of going to gay bars and adult bookstores where he could have impersonal sex with men. Glenn knew that his choice for a life-style was truly heterosexual, but felt cursed by his addiction. As his addiction abated, he was able to increasingly enjoy his relationship with his wife. This is quite different from Ryan, whose genuine choice of a mate would have been another man, and his choice of addictive acting out was also men. Electing a female spouse was based on fear of the oppression he would be subject to if he were "out."

So long as the cross-wiring exists, both the person and the opposite sex partners will know something is wrong. Sexual energy belongs inside the chosen relationship, not outside, and will create natural jealousy for the mate.

THERE ARE MANY OTHER ISSUES

I have described above many of the stories that I have heard in my practice, and there are countless more. Each couple brings together a unique set of obstacles to loving each other with healthy sexual energy. If you and your mate don't want the same amount of sex or the same kinds of sexual activities, there is something going on that prevents you from discovering sex as a natural unfolding and bonding process. Using the methods presented in the following chapters can help you and your mate to uncover your story and work together to change its effects.

There is hope for couples to learn together what their healthy sexual expression is. It requires dedication to emotional healing and the willingness to say everything and hear everything. If you haven't seen your story here, please tell it yourself. *Total honesty with safe people is necessary in order to open the channels to intimacy.* The remaining chapters address things you can do to open the doors to discovering that you and your mate want the same frequency of sex and the same sexual activities. When you are able to clear the way for them, your bodies will make your decisions.

Chapter 5

Creating a Sexual Moratorium

I have noticed in working with people on sexual issues that when a person is recovering from sexual addiction, childhood sexual abuse or cross-wired use of sexual energy, a natural part of the process entails a lengthy period of celibacy. This is often frightening because of our cultural myth that sexual people want sex on a regular basis. To the contrary, it seems to be necessary to give up old kinds of sex before we discover the new ones. We are so bound up with old rules and habits that a period of relating with one's partner without sex offers an amazing education—one that is not available in any other way.

If the partner doesn't understand the change process when someone is in sexual recovery and interest in old sex falls away, he or she may be distressed. Calling a moratorium on sex can be useful if one person feels the need to stop sex, even if the other doesn't. Agreeing to stop being sexual for a period can allow feelings to emerge, which are then available to deal with. For example, if a sex addict who was addicted to sex with his wife suddenly stops asking for sex and seems uninterested in it, his wife is going to react. Identifying the need for a break in the old ways of being sexual before the new arrive can help make sense of the change.

No Sex

No sex! This idea doesn't usually occur to couples unless they are old or sick. The rule is that you must have sex if you are in a relationship. If you don't want to "make love," something is wrong with you, and your partner is entitled to leave or seek sex elsewhere. These rules prevent people from discovering how their sexuality was damaged in a way that now inhibits its natural expression. I suggest that you and your mate agree to go without sexual stimulation as a first step in opening yourselves to new sexuality.

Sexual healing, and the steps described in the remaining chapters, can happen without a sexual moratorium. Some couples have already disengaged themselves from the obligatory rules, and are ready for the process of bringing new sex into their lives. If you or your mate find yourselves resistant to the idea of stopping sex for a time, it might be a further indication to try it.

Defining the Moratorium

1. How long?

Setting a time limit on a moratorium prevents it from working as well as it might. With a set time, each person knows that at a given point, sex will be back, and perhaps with no change. A time limit causes both people to live for the future, either with fear or anticipation. Focus on the future prevents being in the present—one major objective of the moratorium.

If you view a sexual moratorium as an adventure, a time to learn something entirely new and as yet undefined, then it isn't possible to know now when you will be ready for the next step.

I have noticed that couples begin a moratorium believing that it won't go on more than a few weeks, but as time passes, it becomes clear to them that the lessons must take longer. Several months to several years seems to be more typical before being ready to move on.

2. What does "no sex" mean?

You and your partner can discuss the definition of "no sex" as it applies to your relationship. For some, it means no stimulation of genital areas, for others the moratorium includes kissing. For still others, giving up their sexual relationship might mean sleeping in different beds for a time, and not being together without clothes. As you decide what it means for you, ask yourself what your problem areas are. If hugs feel intrusive to one partner, then hugs can be included in the moratorium.

One way to find out what activities to abandon is to ask yourself what it would take to feel free with your mate. It might be OK to have pats on the back, but no hand holding. Anything you feel constrained to do, or not to do, can be put in the off limits category. In the beginning, you might want to put many things on that list, knowing that when you are both ready, you will reclaim them as acceptable. The moratorium doesn't have to be all or nothing. Rather, it is a time to be curious and experiment, discovering the issues that you want to learn more about.

3. What is the "drug" you are putting on hold?

Your moratorium may include more than sexual activity. Romantic actions that act as a drug to either of you can be set aside for now. For example, when Maggie left a love note for Richard, he spent the day reading it and feeling loved and special. He later saw that it was a drug because he wasn't in the present with Maggie. Of course he worried that she wouldn't still be in that place eight hours later. If the note weren't a drug, he would have been able to know that when she wrote it she felt loving, and that at the end of the day she would feel something else— something he would be curious to learn about. Richard and Maggie decided to forego love notes until they were no longer a drug to either one.

Cuddling at night is a wonderful way for couples to bond and feel closer to each other. Yet for Richard and others, even that had to be put on hold. When cuddling is contaminated by the reassurance of love, or is given out of pressure to give reassurance, then it isn't loving.

Hazel and Henry didn't give up hugging. It was wonderful to hug at night with no expectation of sex because it allowed Henry to find out that he felt loved anyway. Hazel felt physically loving with Henry because she no longer felt pressured to respond to hugs by having sex. You and your mate will have to decide what role hugging and cuddling plays in your moratorium. Its role may change from time to time.

4. What about masturbation?

I recommend learning how to "make love to yourself," as part of your sexual healing. This is covered in Chapter 9. But it's entirely up to you when to undertake this part of healing. You may want to give up masturbation at the same time you stop sex with your mate, or you may want to stop them at different times. At some point I encourage you to give up masturbation as you know it now because it breeds shame—the shame that became cross-wired to it when you first discovered how to touch yourself, and later when you began to have orgasms. If you discover that you are using masturbation to substitute for sex with your mate, then giving it up will be helpful to the process you are undertaking.

If you are a recovering sex addict, then you already know you can't masturbate as you did. You know that it will encourage your acting out, and that it makes you feel bad about yourself and even more likely to act out. Please read about the healthy kind of self-touching in Chapter 9. It won't bring on addiction or increase negative attitudes toward yourself.

WHAT HAPPENS WHEN PEOPLE STOP HAVING SEX?

Every story of sexual moratorium is unique. I am continually surprised as I hear new accounts. Here are some of the things people discover when they stop having sex.

1. One partner is sexually addicted

When I suggest a sexual moratorium to a couple, it is striking to me that one person goes crazy. It seems impossible for some people to consider not having sex. Fear of being deprived of the lover's sexual availability is strong. This reaction indicates the likelihood of addiction to sex with the partner. The intense reaction parallels the fears of alcoholics when they are asked to stop drinking.

Michael and Eileen came to my couples workshop on sexuality because Michael was unable to have erections, and was using injections into his penis to create them in order to have sex. Their therapist had been unable to help Michael with his "problem," and so she referred him to me.

During the workshop it became clear that Eileen had intense reactions when she couldn't have sex with her husband. She told us emphatically that she was a very sexual person, and that she was being deprived of expressing this part of herself if he didn't have sex with her. As I began to see that she had the desperation of an addict, I suggested a moratorium from sex until they were able to sort out what was going on. Her desperation increased, and she raged at me and at Michael.

For several weeks, the moratorium was one way. Michael was able to see that he had to stop forcing himself to have sex so he could learn what his penis was trying to communicate by refusing erections. He told Eileen that he was not going to have sex for a time, and that he had to do this for his own sexual healing. He needed my weekly support to prevent himself from giving in to her "logical" reasons why he shouldn't be depriving her of sex.

In a few weeks, however, Eileen's work with her own therapist helped her see that Michael must have time off from sex in order to learn about his sexuality. She was able to forgo her drug, and support Michael in his explorations of childhood sexual abuses, but she didn't yet grasp that her own sexuality wasn't healthy.

Michael's self-esteem grew rapidly as he was able to see that sexual "performance" had nothing to do with his worth. He was delighted to know that sexual health required saying no to sex when it wasn't an expression of intimate caring. In a few months he fully knew that he would never have sex again unless it felt right for him to do so. His energy level increased and his business improved.

Michael was now able to turn lovingly toward his wife because he no longer felt responsible for her oppressive desire for sex. By being able to refuse any time he felt pressure, he eventually felt sexual when they hugged and kissed. By this time, Eileen had agreed to the moratorium (although she was willing to end it at any time), so she was putting no pressure on Michael.

Trina and Monty had a different experience when deciding not to have sex. Monty had relied on sex with Trina to feel loved, and as a result she had grown to hate it. They made a decision together, before coming to see me, that they had to end their painful dance by agreeing not to have sex for a time. Monty discovered that he was addicted to sex with Trina, and found it painful to give up his drug. At the same time, he was greatly relieved to end the struggle. He knew Trina lied to him constantly about her reasons for not wanting sex, and implied that he was defective for wanting it so much. Now they were able to set aside the struggle and make room for understanding.

Monty immediately began to explore what was going on with him when he wanted to have sex, so he could see the motivation for his addiction. Among his discoveries was the realization that Trina had a special, sexually charged relationship with their daughter that made him feel jealous and left out. Now that he didn't try to use sex to eliminate his jealousy he was able to give feedback to Trina when she was acting inappropriately with their daughter. At the same time, she was able to receive this information. The relationship among all three improved.

When Trina and Monty prepared to give up their moratorium and learn how to become sexual again, Monty was filled with fear. He enjoyed the comfortable affection they now had, and was afraid of going back to the old ways. It was helpful to them when I suggested they need never go back to the old ways. I offered suggestions about how they might begin again with sex as if they were adolescents in a healthy culture.

2. Love is not based on sex

Our culture is fraught with beliefs about sex that interfere with understanding its real purpose. Among them are the following:

✦ Having sex is "making love."
✦ If someone wants us sexually we are wanted in the most powerful way possible.
✦ Agreeing to have sex when our partner wants to proves our love.
✦ We are seen as a couple if we are having sex or at least sharing sexual energy.

When a couple gives up sex they get to find out how they really feel about each other. Intimacy can happen to people sitting across from each other, not touching, while talking openly about feelings and experiences.

Henry had believed that sex was a necessary component of his love for Hazel, and her love for him. He had been a loner before meeting her in college, and when he suggested they get married, it was because he knew he couldn't stop having sex with her. He didn't know what else he valued in being with her. As a result, when she found sex obligatory and began to enjoy it less, he was frightened. More had been going on than he knew. Lying in bed, holding Hazel and finding her more loving than she had been when he expected regular sex, he came to enjoy the moratorium. He was able to feel love for her, and to be loved by her, without the method he thought was necessary. The moratorium changed his life. He discovered what love is. He was able to feel a deep commitment to be with Hazel.

3. Relief

Those who have struggled to pull away from a partner who wanted sex for reassurance, or for addiction, are relieved not to be engaged any longer in the struggle. Addicts can also feel relieved after a time, because they can no longer pursue the drug in the form of sex with a mate. Ending the struggle opens both people to something new.

Hazel felt tremendous relief when Henry stopped communicating with his face and body that he needed his fix. She was also relieved of the pressures that came from having internalized the values of our culture.

Daniel felt an initial reluctance to give up his pursuit of Emily, but soon both felt the relief from years of constant conflict, alleviated briefly by sex—sex that left Emily feeling violated. Now they could love each other, reduce their conflict and neither was violated by sex that didn't serve to bond them as a couple.

4. Fear

Most people I work with feel frightened at the prospect of entering a sexual moratorium—even those who might derive the greatest relief. Some fear that the partner now has permission to fantasize, masturbate and have sex with others; usually they are the partner of sex addicts. Some fear there will be no substance left to the marriage. Still others fear losing hold over the addicted mate, and worry that the mate will discover that this isn't how he or she really wants to live. Partners of sex addicts often have a difficult time withdrawing the drug because it is one control they have over the addict. When addicts divest themselves of their perceived need for a drug, they are literally freer to live life as they choose. This can feel threatening to a partner.

George went into a panic when I told him that a moratorium seemed necessary so that he and Grace could discover what role sex was playing in their relationship. He told me I was wrong to suggest this, and that his sex addiction did not extend to sex with Grace. His distress level was a good indicator that his addiction included sex with Grace, particularly when he told me he feared acting out sexually if he was cut off from pursuing sex with her. For a time he did find it difficult not to act out. He flirted with attractive women in his office, and went to a topless club to be brought to orgasm manually.

Grace was frightened also. Even though she felt relief from the pressure to take care of George with sex, she was also frightened of the implications of his acting out. With her knowledge that it was truly best for her to stop having sex and to remove the requirement to have sex from marriage, she sensed that everything would change. It did. As time went on, she and George both could see that the moratorium was for the better.

5. Sexual feelings are just sexual feelings

Being in a relationship without being sexual may give you your first chance to discover what sexual feelings are like when they aren't seen as the forerunner to sexual activity, or as the source of frustration when sexual activity isn't forthcoming. We are sexual beings, and we will have sexual feelings flowing around inside of us when it is right for them to do so. A moratorium, and an examination of cross-wiring, give us a chance to learn what this is like. I have heard several people try to describe how different it feels to be aware of their sexuality without any goal and without sexual feelings being oriented to their mate or to anyone else. In this sexually repressed and sexually overstimulated culture, our usual experience of sexuality is made up of reaction to stimuli. *As we inhabit a quiet place with our sexuality, we can discover that the feeling isn't hard and quick, but rather gently powerful, opening and spiritual.* Sexuality doesn't require that anything be done, just experienced.

6. We get a chance to start over

All of us were awkward when beginning to express sexuality with ourselves and others. The shame was loaded on us long before puberty, and we weren't allowed to talk about sex in open, informative ways. Our sexuality had been so repressed that it became reactive to any stimuli that would allow it to jump out so we could experience it. This took the form of lust or romance or yearning, and created a longing for someone with whom we could share these feelings. *Even the best stories of first sexual encounters include shame and secrecy.* None of us got to have them openly and with our family's support.

A moratorium on sex, and an accompanying exploration of sexual issues, followed by the gradual introduction of sexual activity as explained in Chapter 9, can allow you and your mate to begin again. History doesn't have to repeat itself. As you create a new sexual arena together, you can undo the effects of the first time around.

The next chapter describes what it might have been like to grow up in a sexually healthy culture, perhaps offering an idea of what you and your mate can create for yourselves.

Chapter 6

Growing Up In A Sexually Healthy Culture

I would like to propose a picture of what healthy evolution of sexuality might look like for a person born into a healthy culture. You might envision yourselves growing up again in a culture that allows you to explore your sexuality without shame and on your own time schedule.

The story could begin like this:

You are born fully sexual. Sexual potential and sexual feelings are a natural part of your developing sense of yourself, along with the desire to live, to be taken care of and loved.

As your mother offers a breast for nourishment, she delights in her ability to feed you from her body. Her feelings about her breasts are free from shame. When others watch her feed you, they do not have sexual thoughts about her breasts, but see them as beautiful organs for feeding a new being. Your mother hasn't had years of regarding her breasts as sexual objects for the arousal of men. She respects and understands the sexual feelings her breasts can have. She doesn't have feelings of worth based on breast size, or on the power of attracting attention, that she can pass on to you. She doesn't experience you as a lover because you suck on her breast. Your feelings about breasts are clean and appreciative. You meet your need for food with feelings of calm and pleasure for both of you.

Your parents focus their sexual energy into their relationship, and have none left over to spill accidentally onto you. As you go through the dependent stage of life, when adults carry you everywhere, bathe and dress you, you feel safe and secure that they attend only to your needs; they do not use you for needs they're not meeting elsewhere.

First Sexual Feelings

When you are old enough to walk, and you see your parents being sexual with each other, which they do in many of their day-to-day interactions, you might invite yourself to join them in a hug. They could continue to have sexual feelings toward each other, but these feelings are kept separate from their feelings toward you. They can be sexual with each other without arousing your sexuality. Your arousal comes from inside of you, when you are curious about this part of being human. When your other needs are met—when you aren't hungry or sleepy or needing affection—you might explore these other feelings. One of those times might be when you see adults having sexual feelings with each other. Their use of sexual energy might make you think of yours, and if the time is right, then you might explore. You could touch your genitals and see how the feelings increase.

When you are around three you will find that your interest in sexual feelings and in your genitals becomes stronger. Other maturational needs are pretty well taken care of now. You can walk, talking is getting easier, and you are feeling quite separate from your parents—a real individual. Now you have room to attend to your sexual self. If you are a boy, you want to show off your penis. You want others to see that it changes size, and that when it is larger it usually has more feeling in it. You want people to be delighted with you when you take off your clothes and run around with it bobbing up and down. If you are a girl, you might touch your genitals and look at them. You could rub against a parent, tipping your head while looking adoringly, and smiling.

You live in a respectful home where parents and siblings understand that your sexual feelings are a delight to you. They won't see your sexual expression as an invitation for them to have their own arousal or to join you in sexual activity. They will observe, and be delighted with your delight, as will the neighbors and other adults when you show yourself off to them.

Relatives will mention to you that a few people were sexually damaged as they were growing up, and they may want to be sexual with you. Your parents will calmly explain that they want to know if anyone wants to touch you in ways that don't feel right. They need only tell you briefly because you already know when touch feels healthy, and so of course you will know when it is intrusive. Your parents have listened to all your other distresses, so you know you can take something like this to them too, and be heard. If someone does touch you in a way that doesn't feel right, you may be frightened, but you know someone is close by to protect you. If the person who touches you intrusively is a parent, you tell another relative, who immediately protects you from further violation. You are not left alone with the parent until she or he has seen a therapist and is able to touch you in ways that are healthy.

After a time you will become curious about this sexual rela-tionship between your parents. It looks interesting, and you know that you, too, might want to have one when you are grown up, much as you are becoming aware that you want to do other things they do—driving a car, going to work, cooking and having your own family. So you flirt with one of them. You put all your sexual energy into trying to attract his or her attention, to get him or her to bond with you, instead of bonding with your other parent. This is pretty serious business, like learning to walk and having to work on the balance part of it over and over until you get it right. But this turns out differently. No matter how hard you try, your parent won't break the bond with the other parent, and won't create a monogamous bond with you. This is very frustrating. Eventually you realize that it won't work, and you give up. It becomes clear that this is like driving and going to work—you have to wait until you grow up some more before you can do it. You have a glimmer of awareness that you will bond with someone else—someone who also doesn't have a sexual bond, and who wants one. No point in trying again with someone who is already bonded.

The thought goes through your head that perhaps a sibling is available—someone who doesn't already have a bond. As soon as the thought appears, you reject it. No, not with them! But friends seem a little more interesting. You might talk to your friends about things you have seen your parents do, like kissing and hugging. It feels good when you try it, so you go on to explore those other parts of your bodies that you already knew brought good feelings. You see what penises and vaginas and labia and testicles look like. You find out what it feels like to have them touched by someone else. You may do this with several friends, some of each sex, and find out how different genitals can look, and how different it can feel to be touched by various children. Your curiosity may focus intensely in this area of humanness for a time, before moving on to your next developmental task.

As you learn about these things over a period of months, you tell your parents all about it. They listen with interest in the same way they have about anything new you are learning. You might tell your mother that you saw Rachel's labia today, and they were much bigger than Deborah's. You might say, "Mommy, why are some labia big and others are small?" Or, "Why can I see my penis's head but Victor has skin over his?" Your siblings may tell what they learned when they were your age, and compare stories. This is really fascinating stuff. Your parents respond in the same interested, alive way they do when you tell about learning how to read an entire book, or being able to swim all the way across the pool.

When you have learned enough about all of this, then it is time to move on to skills that will serve you as you become an adult. Sports are one way to learn, reading another. You may find one area that interests you more, or be drawn to several at the same time. Now your life will move toward going places and doing things, and sexuality will fall into the background until it is time for it again. No one will be deliberately arousing you. Otherwise it will be difficult to let sexual energy make its own choices as to when and where it will emerge. The people in your life know that your sexuality will unfold when it is your time. Your age mates will not be feeling very sexual either, and those who are already reaching puberty won't see you as an interesting potential sex partner because it isn't time for you to join in this new process.

PUBERTY

When you reach puberty, however, everything changes. Now the younger kids who are still in sexual latency won't be very interesting, and those who are also going through hormonal changes will become fascinating. It seems like from one day to the next, several other people around your age have become different. Instead of a person with a name and some predictable characteristics, you now see someone who intrigues you. Actually, you see several such people, and are drawn to them as if a magnet had appeared under your skin and theirs. You find that some of your interests are put on hold for a while, or at least don't pull at you with the same strength. Your desire to explore has changed its focus.

Your teachers are prepared for this change. They mirror back to you some of your shock that previous interests seem of little value, and that your curiosity is now so focused on other people.

School changes to meet your needs, with less direction in academic pursuits and more in the personal. In sex education, the role of intercourse in conception is made clear. Educators know it is only a matter of time until you experiment with sexual activity. They know that intercourse must no longer be connected with pregnancy, as it once was, and on the heels of puberty, because our world has changed. Now when a heterosexual couple have established themselves in their work lives and their home, they are in a better position to welcome their babies a decade later than they might have in the past. Same sex couples don't have to worry about this. They choose when to have babies, calling on the many models for how to do this.

The next years are chaotic in some ways as you explore with others how to select a mate. You find that two things are happening. You feel sexual a lot now. Your peers and teachers understand what is happening because talk is open. For boys, erections seem to come unbidden, and sometimes orgasms do, too. Everyone knows that when a young man has a bulge in his pants, his sexual energy is practicing for when he is ready to use the erection for sexual pleasure with a lover or self-touch. It is so common that people hardly notice it after the first few times. Those early erections are a male's initiation into his adult sexuality.

For girls, the ability to have strong sexual arousal is accompanied by the beginning of menstruation. The first flow of red is celebrated, as your family and friends join in the excitement over your new status as a young woman. You have become able to use your body to invite new life. You already know there are several ways to catch the blood because you have seen other women do so from the time you were a baby. You are familiar with the reverence around this blood, the knowing that it is the food for embryos as they become babies. You feel no disgust or fear because it is familiar. You may already have seen births.

Your community helps you discover the form you want your celebration to take. Some young women will use menstrual blood in a ceremony, while others may focus on the babies to be invited. Long before the beginning of menstruation and erection, males and females are prepared for these physical changes and for the appearance of pubic hair, changes in body shape and emotional upheaval. You know what to expect because your older siblings or neighbors have been through it. Everyone talks about it, much as they mention who is getting married and when babies are on the way. There is no mystery, no secrecy and no shame about the natural change from one stage of life to the next.

To honor your transition into adulthood, there is a ritual. You select the activities that are used to acknowledge the change. The rituals used in the past, and your own creativity, are available for a celebration that has significance for you.

FINDING A PARTNER

Now the longer process of learning about the function of sexual energy in finding a partner and bonding into a unit begins. You interact with several of the people you are drawn to, and spend more time getting acquainted. With some of these people you know quickly that, while sexual feelings might be strong, mating is not possible. These interactions diminish. When a person you really like seems to share your life interests, holds similar values and really likes you too, and sexual attraction is strong, then you continue to explore together.

Sexual energy is already part of your relationship because you have chosen each other on the basis of partnering interest—an interest that is fueled by sexual energy. Whether you spend hours looking into each other's eyes, or engage in intercourse, you are beginning the process of bonding yourselves into a couple. Even if you are both thirteen years old, and not wishing to marry and have children, the emotional process is the same as it would be if you were twenty-six and ready to begin a family. You understand this process is inherent in being human, and you honor it. You know it would be foolish to be sexual more than a few times with a person you don't want to partner with, because you would bond together anyway. The choice to bond is not one made by the intellect.

When you find a person you feel compatible with, then you may be ready to explore sexual activity. You find that sexual energy opens you up, and removes the usual boundaries of privacy and modesty. These boundaries, important in creating a sense of your separate self, are not useful now, when the task is finding out how to have oneness. You find this experience joyful and exhilarating. Your life tasks have had much to do with separating yourself from family members for many years. Now you get to return to the primitive experiences of your infancy. Naked and open, looking deeply into each other's eyes and souls, and aroused by the power of sexuality so that your skin and organs vibrate, you come into possession of a new life.

You curiously explore each other, finding out how your body works and how your partner's works. You learn how to bring on strong arousal in yourself and in your partner, and see the function this has in enhancing the opening and bonding. You discover that your bodies know exactly what to do, and turn yourselves over to them. You have sex often, and you tell others about it. As you hear their stories, this new part of humanness becomes more natural. In time, being a sexual person in a relationship becomes an accepted, understandable part of your life.

You may find your mate quickly, or you may go through a series of matings as each one of the early matches doesn't turn out to be a lifetime coupling. In this latter case, the two of you must grieve for the loss of intense bond that sexual energy has created before you are able to move on to your next choice. This grieving process is very intense. To break the bond, it has to be equal in force to the power of sexual energy that created it. The grief is as painful as the sexual bonding was pleasurable. But you are able to complete the grief process in a few weeks because you have complete access to your emotions, and can let the anger and tears flow. You already know how they do their job because you have had other losses to deal with, either permanent or temporary, during your earlier years.

You may find that you have periods without a partner, as you return to other interests. This becomes possible as you get used to your adult sexual energy and it is no longer new and chaotic.

Masturbation might play a role in your life, too. Your first explorations of how your sexual body works will include touching yourself sexually to learn about your body parts, what they do and how orgasm happens. You may delight in making love to yourself. At the same time, you also know that this energy is designed to bond you to another person, and so your attention is usually outward. Your radar can perceive the broadcasts of those who want mates, particularly if you want one too. You may find your attention drawn more to one gender, or to both genders equally.

You don't have to deal with people trying to ensnare you into a sexual relationship if you are securely bonded. If you are bonded, you will send that message out (much as you saw your parents weren't available to you because they were bonded with each other). Others who aren't bonded will know that you aren't one of the possibilities, and so won't waste their sexual energies in your direction.

BONDING WITH YOUR MATE

When you find a mate, and everything seems to be right for being together, then sexual energy will bond you. In the beginning, perhaps the first few times you are together and using sexual energy, it will feel delightful. The bond starts to form, but your sexuality may still find other available people interesting. Neither of you feels jealous of the other's interest in another. But in a matter of several weeks you go through a change. Seemingly from one day to the next, you find that you don't want your partner to send sexual energy to someone else. You want it all for yourself. Your partner is delighted with your feelings, and expresses joy. At the same time, you find that your sexual interest in other people is dropping rapidly. When you meet a person who is available, and with whom you had exchanged sexual energy only a few weeks before, you will find that your sexual energy is not engaged. This is information to you that you are mating, and you might feel even more joyful as you tell your partner about it. As each of you affirms how your sexuality is limiting itself to the other, your bond strengthens.

As weeks become months, your lives mingle further, and you feel like a couple. After a time, the bonding feels complete, and you find that your attention is no longer drawn so intensely to each other. Instead, your old interests and friends resurface, only now to be integrated into your mated relationship. You jostle some priorities, perhaps with some fear and jealousy as each of you is concerned with maintaining the bond. But in a few more months you see how both the relationship and the rest of your lives can mesh to provide richness that far exceeds each facet.

Sexual activity assumes less importance in your life now. It has done its job of creating a new family. While you still feel a sexual hum when relating intimately with your partner (with or without sexual activity) the urge to take it farther has lessened. You warmly and joyfully expand into each other when the time is right—when you can dedicate yourselves to each other fully. The purpose is to rebond, a regular need that surfaces after each of you has oriented to other needs for a time. Now you have the leisure to explore each other more quietly, with less urgency. The experience of sexuality continues to expand as you learn more and more about this powerful energy. Your sexual lessons continue throughout your life. You can't learn them all right away. As the two of you go on learning, you find yourselves always curious, and never knowing what lessons will appear each time. This process can never be boring, even with the same partner and similar sexual activities.

By now you have moved well into the complex process of "marrying." The wedding ceremony is only a ritual that affirms a natural process with several facets. The sexual bonding and sexual activity components are complete. Another is living in the same home, and yet another the mingling of finances. At some point during this process you may find that you know throughout yourself that this is your life mate. Then a wedding is useful to announce to your community that you are a couple. You use the power of standing up in front of other people and stating to each other in words and gestures that you are together—perhaps for life. You find that the public statement makes you feel even more bonded. The ritual allows more of your being to know that you are together. As well, others in your community now see you as a couple, and reflect this back to you, further affirming your mating. If you add children, their presence further bonds you by creating a family in which the two of you are responsible.

If you should decide to break your bond, then the process reverses itself. Sexual energy is cut off so that it no longer holds you together. Intense feelings of grief replace intense feelings of joy—emotions necessary to change our perception of the past so that it corresponds to the present. You find yourself in rages, screaming out your pain of loss. At times if may seem that life isn't worth living because you felt half of a whole, and now the other half isn't there. Other times you sob, in effect cleansing yourself deeply. The process is intense. Your employer, friends and family make room for it, expecting that you won't be as attentive as you usually are to other tasks and relationships. They know that if they support your grief, it will soon pass and leave you again with plenty of energy and attention for other parts of your life. They are aware that mating is deeply significant, and the community supports it, both in the creating of the bond and in the breaking of it.

You know that while you are separating from your mate it is not time to look for another. It isn't possible to experience the joy of new bonding fully while in the anguish of breaking the old. It isn't a conscious decision. You see that your sexual energy doesn't re-emerge, and trust that it will when the time is right, after the grief is complete. You may also enjoy a period of being single, exploring this life-style again, falling in love with yourself.

Then one morning you wake up and suddenly there are many attractive, available people around. You begin again the process of sorting, as they sort, until you find a new mate.

If your last bonding included having children, you are now in a position of parenting without a mate. As you send out your sexual energy, you find it possible to regulate it so that you do not direct it at your children or toward people who are in relationships. Actually, it never occurs to you to send your energy in these directions because they are not areas in which you will find a mate. The only fruitful place to direct it is toward those who are also available.

Your mated friends, remembering their mating days, want to find unmated people for you to sort with. They know that you will need to meet many before finding the right match, and they want to help once they see you are ready. At this later time in life most people around you are already mated, and so your community helps to bring together those who aren't. Eventually you find a person, one who is even more suited to you. You are older, and know more about your needs in a mate, as your mate knows her or his needs too.

You again move into a mated state. As you settle into marriage, it feels correct. There is something right about merging your life with the life of another. You have learned how to do it without overdoing it. You sacrifice nothing of yourself to have a mate and children. Meeting responsibilities is joyful because it is right for you. Everything you do in your life is from choice because you can clearly see what brings you the richest life, and so all your decisions are useful ones. Even bonding and then breaking the bond make sense in the scheme of your life.

SEX OVER THE YEARS

Your bonding matures over a few years, and the need for sex to re-bond or to invite children becomes a normal, understandable part of life. If one of you is focused away from the relationship, the other isn't interested in sex either. When it is time to re-bond, then both of you find sex compelling.

Couples have differing patterns of sexual activity over the years. Sometimes you may enjoy sexual feelings when touching, but only occasionally go on to intercourse and orgasms. Other times you have intercourse frequently. Less interest is based on many things. If you are securely bonded you enjoy sex together, but it isn't necessary. It is simple. Sometimes you have sex, other times you don't. There are no rules because rules would limit the free expression of yourselves and your bonded relationship.

A ceremony is held by women when menstruation stops. You express the feelings that come up as your flow changes, and grieve for the loss of fertility. Looking at yourself intently, you notice how different you appear after only a very few years. Getting acquainted with the new you, and accepting yourself, is assisted by the loving looks and touches you receive from your mate. Your partner's touch feels just as loving and accepting, reminding you that you are the same person. The only difference is that you are entering a new place in the life cycle, one that brings freedom from responsibilities of younger years, and wisdom accumulated from living fully. Sexuality affirms your life in a changing body, and your continuing bond with your mate.

Men also change during the middle years. Your body is becoming different too. You are softer and rounder as lines and wrinkles form. As your mate's body changes shape, you touch her frequently to allow your hand to know that she is the same person, and to remind yourself that the bond is still there, ever maturing. As you run your hand over drier skin, and notice the change in her vagina, and feel her rounded belly, you rejoice in the years you have had together, and the knowledge of the years to come. You cry with her to release the attachment to both your bodies as they had been. In the middle years your interest changes from the firm, muscled bodies of youth to the ones you now reside in. The softness of her skin feels electric to your hands, and the years of fitting the two of you together helps you adjust to the change. Sex serves as a reminder of the formlessness of your love.

As the decades move you into old age, your sexual patterns may change many times, reflecting your emotional and physical states. Even when you aren't being sexual, your sexual energy flows as strongly as ever, keeping you alive and bonded. Your children and grandchildren know you are a sexual person, even if you are wrinkled and move slowly. It is expected that people will be sexual whenever they feel like it, and that age does not limit the full expression of sexuality. We are sexual beings.

Note: This chapter, and chapter 11, are also available on an audio cassette called *Healthy Sex: Real Life Stories of Bonding, Monogamous, Joyful, Shame-Free, Rule-Free Sex,* read by the author, available at your local book store or through the publisher.

Chapter 7

Learning About Each Other's Feelings

Sexual healing with your mate requires safety in order to be open and vulnerable with truths that are painful to reveal, and perhaps painful to hear. Hurt feelings, blaming and pointless circular fights that cannot resolve anything will interfere with revealing your experience. Yet the whole truth must be told if you are to embark on complete sexual healing. (You may want a therapist's help if the feelings get more intense than you feel able to handle.)

The premise underlying your work together is that *each of you is responsible for your own feelings.* Your partner cannot take responsibility for making changes to avoid evoking certain feelings in you.

While feelings are not caused by your partner, he or she may be doing something that triggers them in you, and perhaps even wants unconsciously to cause them. *So long as you hold the other person responsible, you cannot discharge your feelings and change your reactions.* It helps to know that you are not the victim of someone else's behavior, that you can take action to change how you feel.

This is not to say that your partner is innocent and you are making everything up. He or she may be doing some pretty awful things that may be hurtful and may provoke justifiable reactions. If so, you get to make changes for yourself, rather than wait for your partner to change so that you'll feel better.

SHEDDING FEELINGS FROM THE PAST

One thing you can do is to create an arena where you may express all your rage or fear or hurt. By cleaning out the intense emotions sufficiently, you'll be able to see what belongs in the present. Once you separate the present from the past, then it will be clear what to do with your feelings.

One day, when Rex was working in the yard an hour before company was coming, and he hadn't vacuumed the rug as he said he would, I found myself raging. I knew rage wasn't exactly the right feeling for this situation, but nevertheless, here it was. So I stormed out into the yard, and, not minding if the neighbors heard, I asked Rex if I could yell out my feelings. He nodded as he turned to face me, giving me his full attention.

I started yelling about how he never did anything he said he would, and now here we were expecting people to come and see how we live, and the vacuuming wasn't done. Couldn't he ever do what he said? As I continued, the rage dropped down to anger, and then to annoyance. Finally I began to laugh as I saw how absurd I sounded, and he joined in. In hysterics, we wondered what the neighbors made of our yelling followed by laughter.

Now that I was clear of the old feelings from childhood and earlier adult years, I could see that my feelings had nothing to do with Rex. In truth, I didn't care if the rug was vacuumed. My house felt wonderfully welcoming to anyone I invited there. It took me days to learn that the feelings were about having these particular people in my house. I had invited them without realizing that I didn't want to share my home with them. I had re-directed the feelings onto Rex.

Other times, Rex has done something that I don't like and don't want him to do again. If my feelings are clear of the past, then I know the truth and I express it firmly and lucidly. But if the feelings are contaminated by the past, then I need to clear out those feelings first so I can see the truth.

For example, there are times when Rex walks away from me in a store as if I don't exist. I know he has patterns that tell him he is alone again, that I don't want to be with him, and that he must protect himself by feeling alone before I can abandon him. Yet when it happens, I don't remember that very well. Instead, I am enraged by the times in childhood when I was left to take care of myself while my mother shopped for the perfect outfit and accessories, and the many times my first husband acted as if I weren't with him when we were in stores, and how I was unable then even to mention my hurt and anger.

I let Rex know I am angry. I bark like a dog (our signal that the other is in a pattern from the past and is to take a look at it). With his attention, I snarl (quietly if we are in public!) my anger about how he always abandons me and I may as well wait in the car, and I know he never wanted me along, anyway. If his historic patterns aren't too strong, he turns and gives me good attention, usually smiling. If the patterns are commanding him, then he may have a hard time hearing me. Either way, after I express my anger, and demand that he not abandon me, it becomes clear to me exactly what I do want to ask of him. I tell him firmly that we are married, we are shopping together and I don't want him to go off without me. Whether he hears or not,

I have taken my own authority back instead of reacting to his stimulus. *I was able to do that by expressing both the old patterned feelings and the current, appropriate feelings.* This combination is essential because we will always have old feelings mixed in with present ones. It is impossible to sort them out first, then speak only of the present ones, leaving the past aside. Feelings are not subject to logic, and will come up whether or not you decide it is OK. It is possible to "contain" anger so that it is safe to express it in ways that won't harm your partner. Instead, anger can be used to free your body and psyche from memories of past abuse. If you blame your partner for your feelings, it is harmful to you both. Containing the anger allows you to express it in a way that doesn't harm.

"Containers" are a wonderful device for gathering information about the past so you can see what feelings still come from there. Containers make room for the old feelings to be given expression too, to clear the way for the present ones.

I have adapted the method described here from one devised by Harville Hendrix and described in his book, *Getting the Love You Want* (Henry Holt, 1988). I learned this approach from him in 1986. My version differs from Hendrix's as I have adapted it for my own use over the years. (If you want help in learning to use containers, Hendrix has trained therapists around the country. You can find one closest to you by calling The Institute for Relationship Therapy in New York City at 212-410-7712.)

Containers are good to use in cases of jealousy, which is common to many couples. The very real anger makes sense when one's mate is exchanging sexual energy with another person. Most of us also have huge add-ons from past situations that provoked our jealousy and denied us our feelings. Consequently, when our mate flirts, we have two responses. One is the rage from countless such experiences. The other is real anger at the betrayal occurring in front of us.

If the old rage is cleaned out through the use of containers, then it becomes possible to call up appropriate feelings in the present, and to express them clearly to our mate. When old feelings and blaming are not present, our mate is usually able to hear what we have to say. It can feel loving when you say to your partner, unequivocally, that all sexual energy belongs in this relationship, and it is not OK for any of it to be directed elsewhere.

STEPS TO CREATE A CONTAINER

First, when you feel anger, alert your partner. Ask for a container. If it is not possible to do this immediately, set a specific time.

Second, your partner puts on a psychic shield, which is an awareness that he or she didn't cause this anger, is not a bad person and can help you release stored up feelings (generally the most difficult) by listening. Our shame is ever ready to pop up when another is angry with us, and so the shield needs to be strong enough for you to remain open to listening.

Third, you get to yell or snarl your feelings, without having to worry if they are really about your partner.

For example, when I saw Rex lying in a position that elicited my shameful cross-wired sexual arousal, I went into a rage. I asked him for a container, and he agreed. Then I told him he was trying to trick me into feeling sexual and that I hated him for it. After a few more sentences I could see Rex as he is, and know that he wasn't doing this at all. He was just lying comfortably, looking at me. Once my anger had been expressed, and I was able to see that I was avoiding shame, I could feel and discharge the shame. Only then could I learn that he was triggering feelings that had been left over from my father's sexual abuse of me.

If Rex weren't asked to put on his psychic armor, and if he hadn't been able to do so, my anger would have been entirely confusing to him, and quite harmful. It would have looked as though he were being held responsible for my massive attack of intense feelings. Early on, it was hard for me to know the difference because he really seemed to be responsible. I knew that neither of us would know the truth if I weren't able to clean out the old anger and make room for a present-day understanding of what had just happened.

Sometimes our old anger is mixed in with present-day anger that we need to express directly. In this case, a container can help clear out the old, and allow us to see what is truly current.

Mary, a woman who is in therapy with me, is enraged by her husband's attraction to their teenage daughter. He is also in therapy, working on this issue, and is committed to changing. In the meantime, the daughter is in an unhealthy triangle with her parents and in a position of power with her father. I helped Mary to express healthy anger to her husband. Speaking loudly and firmly, I said that his sexual feelings toward his daughter were not acceptable, and that he must stop harming this child.

Mary's feelings went further, however. She wanted to see him as deliberately turning her daughter against her, and hating Mary for her physical "imperfections." She wanted to scream at him for not loving her, for letting her stay alone by herself while the rest of the family went off to have a good time. As she unloaded, we could see what was real from the present, and what was left over from childhood neglect—feelings that were literally locked up in her body. She was then able to express anger that was entirely appropriate to the present situation. Her husband's reaction to her real anger was positive. He felt seen and cared about, and found her anger to be useful in changing his cross-wired attraction to their daughter.

Learning to put on psychic armor is not easy for most people. We are trained to believe we are the cause of others' distress, and so when someone turns on us, our shame emerges. We become defensive in order to reduce our shame, and thus lose sight of the person who is angry. In time, wearing psychic armor can help us view ourselves as fine people who are able to absorb this onslaught to erase the influence of our past. After watching innumerable times when people went from blaming me to gaining some understanding of what was really going on, I have become able to put the armor on easily.

In the beginning, I felt the necessity of re-visiting the anger, making sure the person really saw the difference between me and their feelings. In time, I could see that once a person moves from rage to a new place of emotional understanding, everything but the truth disappears. Now when someone rages at me, I feel as if I am on an adventure, and I get to watch something very special unfold. I do have to put the armor on, however. Otherwise I am likely to say, "Stop, this is abusive," or otherwise protect myself. And if the person isn't doing his or her "work," it would make sense for me to stop the blame and the attack, which aren't good for either of us.

MAGGIE AND RICHARD

Maggie and Richard arrived at our couples' group irritated and glowering. When everyone had checked in, they let us know right away that they were angry with each other and weren't too delighted to be in group. I asked if they wanted to "do" a container—both to deal with their issues and to create a model for the group. They reluctantly agreed.

Maggie asked to go first. Richard spent a few minutes putting on his armor. He prepared himself so he could hear what she said not as blame of him for being a terrible person (even though she currently saw him that way). He needed to see that her statements were a consequence of her childhood that created rage instead of a clean, pure anger that he did, in fact, warrant. When he was ready, he let her know. I reminded him that if his armor slipped, he could ask Maggie to stop for as long as it took to get it back on. He nodded.

Maggie began her attack. She poured out every bad thing he had done or said the past week, her voice conveying intense hatred and condemnation. I kept an eye on Richard to make sure he didn't forget and think this meant he was a bad person. He kept his armor on.

As Maggie's voice increased in volume and rage over twenty minutes or so, I could see other feelings emerging from underneath: betrayal, hurt, sadness, grief. In a few more minutes they were showing on her face, and tears began to run. Richard's face changed from self-protection to compassion. Maggie began to recount the betrayals from childhood and from her present abandonment by her mother. She sobbed out her grief, begging Richard not to leave her. In a few more minutes, she was done with her container, and could see that she was, indeed, angry with Richard, though he was not the cause of the depth of her feelings of betrayal and abandonment.

Richard asked Maggie to put on her armor so he could work on his own feelings. She took a few more minutes to gather herself together after her powerful emotional discharge. (Couples usually do containers in one direction at a time—since we were in group we didn't have the luxury of waiting until later.)

When Maggie's armor was on, she let Richard know. He began to recite criticisms of how she communicated her anger to him. Intellectually he itemized them, dispensing one after another. Maggie's annoyance came through her armor. He stopped, turned to her and said that he needed to let his "offender" speak and he was holding back. Maggie said she knew her armor wasn't strong enough to handle that at present, and so I offered to stand in for her so he could direct his condemning rage.

He spewed injustices that had been done to him. I found that within a minute I had stopped listening to his actual words and heard only the sound emanating from him. I heard a desperate child who had never been heard as he called out angrily. I found myself caught up in his desperation and isolation, deeply touched with compassion. As he saw my face change, he fell into deep sobs, crying out his need to be seen and loved.

As his sobs fell away, he again became aware of Maggie sitting across from him. He said he was afraid to look at her because he didn't know how she felt toward him. Finally he turned and saw the tears in her eyes. She had seen the child who had been abandoned and was desperate for love. Richard asked how she felt and she asked if she could hug him. After the things he had said to her, he was amazed. They stood up and cried together, each one affirming what they had heard the other say, expressing their compassion and love.

The room was filled with tears and joy as we watched these two people embrace each other physically and emotionally. The containers had taken them from old, biting anger and resentment to a new place of seeing each other's pain.

They didn't stay there. Many containers are often necessary to clear out adulterated feelings to make room for pure ones. But now Maggie and Richard had a model for how the process works, and the encouragement of having felt close and intimate when they'd been willing to go through the pain of raging and the pain of listening to rage.

If you and your mate decide to practice containers, I suggest that you begin with small feelings of annoyance, and postpone the major areas of conflict for a time when you feel more comfortable with the process. For example, when Rex wants to go to bed and I know I won't be ready for an hour or so, I have mild feelings about this. I want him to stay up with me even though I know he should sleep when he is ready. If I am being rational, I won't ask him to stay up with me because I don't want to influence his decision. But at the same time, I have feelings that aren't getting to be expressed. If we were just learning to use containers, this would be a good place to begin because the feelings are relatively small.

I might ask Rex to put on his armor. This would communicate that I was about to express feelings and didn't necessarily want him to respond. I could then open up without having to decide if I was "rational," and thus permissible. I might scold him, telling him that he was selfish, that all he could think of was himself, and I didn't matter to him. If he really loved me he would stay up with me another hour.

As I write I can see that these words were used on me when I was a child to get me to respond to the wishes of others and not to act on what was right for me. It also frees me to see more clearly that I just want his company. Perhaps I might go to bed with a book and be with him, or I may decide that I prefer to stay up by myself. But my choice will be free of the wish to change his mind, and the effort of holding that back.

Minor conflicts could be useful to practice this very powerful method. It is clear to Rex that I have no investment in changing him, and his armor stays easily in place. However, if I expressed the same feelings when he didn't have the advantage of the container, he would rightfully be defensive.

I encourage you to discover how to introduce safe fighting into your relationship. It can help with the expression of anger that will come up as you pursue sexual healing, and as you try not to take personally the other feelings your partner will express as you move more deeply into your recovery process. His or her feelings of hurt, betrayal, grief and fear also need an arena so they can be discharged. Since you are the sexual partner, you will be the one present when these feelings are allowed to come up. Developing your psychic armor ahead of time can prepare you to stay present when you are seen as the cause of the feelings. In truth, you will trigger your mate's distress just by being sexual and present, as he or she will trigger yours. *The ability to hear each other without moving into your own distress is the backdrop for using your relationship as a healing medium.*

Chapter 8

Letting Your Skin Communicate

When we touch another person's body, all information about the response to that touch is available to both. When another person touches us, we know everything about the other person's intent and feelings. We also know all about our own reaction. Our language doesn't include descriptions of this process and so most of us aren't aware that it is going on. We can learn.

When your mate touches you sexually, you know his or her intention through your cells. You don't have to look to know if he or she wants to suck your energy out of you, placate you or control you. If you are receiving loving, respectful touch you know that, too. My eyes, trained by living with a perceptive body worker, can recognize the intention of touch yards away. *All the information is there when we let ourselves know that we know.*

Touch may appear to be harmful even when a person is actually touching cleanly. We can be triggered into "remembering" damaging touch from the past, when we had no opportunity to discharge feelings. We can learn, with the help of containers described in the previous chapter, how to clear out feelings from the past so that we can perceive accurately now.

Rex is a Rolfer by profession, and listens with his hands as he works with clients. While teaching a class on deep tissue touch for a massage school, he created a hand out. Among the items are:

1. Let your touch ask questions.

2. Stay in tune with what you are feeling physically.

3. Stay in tune with what you are feeling emotionally.

4. What story is being told by the body you are touching?

5. What is the tissue (body) asking for?

6. Is the tissue pushing you away, letting you in with ease or hesitating, watching you?

7. Are you confused or is the tissue confused?

8. Are you aroused, anxious, sad, tired, impatient? Or is it the tissue feeling these things?

9. Relaxation and fluid movement in the practitioner's body transmits to the client. So does anxiety.

10. Are you relaxed and comfortable? If not, stop work and do what it takes to get there.

11. If you find yourself not breathing during a session, and your client is not either, start breathing more deeply and both your client's body and yours will become more fluid.

12. Breath makes space for movement and change, physically and otherwise.

Good bodyworkers understand these principles and apply them, sometimes without knowing it. Most of us have to relearn these skills we were born with to become conscious of what we are perceiving. (See *Reclaiming Healthy Sexual Energy* for a chaper on different kinds of body work, and how to choose a bodyworker who will not violate you.) When sexual, you know when your mate is touching you from a place of control, addiction, cross-wiring or intimacy. You may not be sensitive to this information if you are in addiction, or having sex out of obligation, but on some level you are recording it.

I would like to suggest that you and your partner work on discovering these abilities before you begin exploring new sex.

PRACTICING TOUCH

Put your hand on your partner's back or shoulders. Notice what you feel on your hand. Is the temperature warm or cold? Do you have feelings emerging? Is sexual energy welcome? If sexual energy isn't welcome, how would it feel to express it?

Does the tissue feel tight and unmoving? Or fluid and warm? Does the tissue lose all integrity or sense of itself? Does it turn to mush? Do you have a sense of little eyes in each cell watching you to see what you are going to do? Rex describes how cells' eyeballs study him when they aren't sure he is safe. When the body definitely doesn't want to be touched it feels as if two hands strongly push his away. When tissue feels safe, it invites his hands in. If his touch is tentative, tissue will yell out to go deeper.

We can consciously identify body communications as we learn to have sex with intimacy. (When we move to the place where our bodies talk between themselves, and we trust them to make decisions about what to do sexually, then we no longer need to know consciously what they are saying to each other. But for now we do.)

You can practice with your mate. Set aside time when you both want to be together, and are willing to be entirely truthful. Then decide who will touch and who will receive.

As you touch, or receive touch, let your senses be open to whatever they discover. There is no correct way to do this, or right outcome. In fact, you may find that you receive no information at all, and the task seems like a failure. It isn't. This exercise invites you to open to a part of your knowing, and it may be some time before the knowing can be translated into conscious thinking. Practicing alerts your inner self that you want this information.

For a long time I knew that Rex knew what went on in my tissues when he touched me. I was also able to listen to my body's response, and feel my cells' eyeballs looking at him suspiciously when they were in distress. I was aware what my skin communicated to him, and what he received. But only recently have I come to see that, even though I am not trained as a bodyworker, I too can describe what tissue is experiencing.

I began with global words, like "tense," "tight" and "soft." Now I have learned that typical phrases that apply to skin can't be counted on to communicate accurately. I had to give up censoring the words my mind wanted to use, no longer judging them as stupid or crazy. If I think in terms of eyeballs or little hands pushing out, it gives me new language to communicate with.

TISSUE EXPRESSIONS

Rex and I came up with "tissue expressions" to assist our understanding of what we know. Some of these are:

♦ Hey, watch it
♦ Get away from me
♦ I'll shrink into a ball so you can't get inside
♦ Ohhhh, yummy

✦ I'm melting into sexual feeling
✦ I have hard sexual arousal
✦ What do you want from me?
✦ I'm watching you
✦ I'll harden up so you can't get in to me
✦ I'm freezing cold
✦ I'm sweating
✦ Hi, there
✦ Come on in
✦ More, more!! Don't stop
✦ Hands off
✦ Don't patronize me
✦ What do you want?
✦ I'm turning to stone
✦ _____(Add your own as you discover them.)

When you put a hand on your partner's back or shoulder, notice which expression your partner's skin seems to be communicating. Then ask your partner to identify his or her experience. When you get close, you know you are listening with your hands. Then reverse roles, and see what your body says when your partner puts his or her hands on you.

SEXUAL SKIN CONTACT

As your touch develops sensitivity, it becomes possible to know what is communicated by your genitals and bodies. The end goal is to allow your bodies to take care of it themselves, but in the meantime you can become conscious of their communication so you can use it to make decisions.

For example, if you touch your partner's penis, the tissue will tell you if this is welcome, if it feels intrusive or if the tissue is moving into cross-wired, addictive response in order to be sexual even against its will.

One morning Rex stood next to me, and I reached out to touch his penis. It immediately responded by filling with blood, expressing its wish to be sexual. As I held it in my hand, I could "read" what Rex was feeling. I described it to him. I said his penis was leaping joyfully up, spreading its arms and basking in the sunshine. He smiled in a way that let me know I was right. I contrasted this response to other reactions his penis communicates, such as the desire to move into my vagina. When that is happening, I know because my vagina is sending out information that she is also interested. This time my genitals didn't join in. The experience was one that belonged to Rex, and was shared with me.

In contrast is my experience with men who could not say no. When the body wanted to say no, but the person could not agree, the penis tissue became hard in a rigid, immobile, demanding style. The physical hardness was not tempered by the flow of energy and communication between his cells and mine.

Cellular communication was demonstrated to me in a recent sexual exchange. Rex and I were touching each other's genitals at the same time. I quickly approached orgasm, and discovered that his penis became especially hard, as it usually does when he is about to have an orgasm—even though I was hardly stimulating it. But when my arousal dropped back, his penis softened, and my hand perceived the change. When I again moved toward orgasm and into it, his penis showed corresponding changes, even though it had no direct contact with my vagina. Once my orgasm was complete, his orgasm refused to be postponed in spite of our conscious wish to have intercourse. When we finally gave in to our bodies' decisions, it became obvious that we were violating his body by insisting the orgasm be delayed.

The truths your bodies can tell each other are inhibited by performance requirements, and other ways you are distracted by things non-sexual. Your bodies take in the information, but are unable to respect it.

BODY WORK CAN HELP

Sexual recovery is greatly assisted by massage, Yoga, Rolfing and other kinds of touch that allow you to experience your self inside your physical form. *Reclaiming Healthy Sexual Energy* offers information about several kinds of body work, and how they can help.

Chapter 9

Making Love to Yourself

S exual self-stimulation, without shame attached, is a valuable way to be sexual. However, most of us have not survived being shamed by our culture and our families. As a result, masturbation as we know it is not healthy. *Every time you climb into the shame compartment, hide yourself from the rest of humanity, and engage in a shameful activity, you are reducing your self-esteem and cutting yourself off from your spiritual knowing.*

Prior to taking the next step to discovering healthy sex, giving up masturbation is advisable. Going for a period without self-stimulation will reduce the shame you have introduced into your life, and allow you to feel better about yourself. It will also let you know that you won't die or become hyper-sexed if you don't have orgasms for a time. As with the moratorium on sex with your mate, the length of this moratorium depends on the lessons you learn from it, and when it feels right to move on in your learning.

Caution to sex addicts: Venture very slowly into the form of self-stimulation I am about to describe. Please be sure you aren't taking this as permission to masturbate in the old ways. If you find any addictive sexual energy emerging, stop, and wait until your addiction recovery is further along before trying again.

The process you can embark on is similar to inviting healthy sexuality when you are ending a moratorium or otherwise preparing to change the way you relate sexually, which is described in the next chapter. Beginning with self-stimulation might allow you to learn about your sexuality without the complication of learning about your mate's at the same time. It also reduces the number of social rules.

Below are some ideas about what to include and omit in your exploration.

1. Don't require arousal

Masturbating the old way means, by definition, that you want to be aroused, and perhaps already are before starting. If you don't get aroused, it isn't considered masturbation. But now, when exploring your body and your sexuality, arousal is not your objective. Your focus is on getting acquainted with yourself, taking care of your body and seeing if your body is interested in arousal.

2. Do not explore when aroused

If you begin this self-loving process when aroused you are likely to be in addiction already, or in cross-wired arousal. Both may prevent you from fully receiving the lessons about a new approach to sexuality. (There may be times when you are learning lessons about the causes of your cross-wiring that you may choose to masturbate while aroused. When you can be sufficiently conscious of what is really happening, lessons may come with the old form of masturbation.)

If you begin without being aroused, you will find more of the shame and fear emerging, which is good. As you allow yourself to feel shame that has been laid thickly upon you since birth, you will be able to let it wash away. If you use the shame compartment to avoid feeling bad, the shame will only cling to you more tightly. One task of sexual healing is inviting the shame to emerge so you can feel it, and this may make self-loving unpleasant for a time. Breathing and letting the shame flow can encourage the release of shame, so you can move on to a joyful arousal.

3. Don't use cross-wired stimuli

Cross-wired stimulation will put you into the shame compartment, remove you from yourself and you will be masturbating in the old way. The result is more locked-in shame. This stimulation can take the form of pornography, fantasy about a person, situation or sexual activities; or a sexual response to something or someone viewed earlier. It can also be a response to feelings of loneliness, shame or yearning. When arousal comes from these experiences, this is not the time to make love to yourself. Rather, begin when you are feeling good and whole, self-loving and curious. Be prepared for no arousal, and allow whatever happens to happen.

4. Don't try for orgasm

The purpose of old masturbation is to get aroused, stay aroused and, finally, to have an orgasm. Removing the end point can help you stay in the present, and change the old programming. If an orgasm happens, unbidden, because your body decided it was time, welcome it and pay attention to it. But avoid "trying" to have one.

5. Don't set goals

Sex and masturbation usually have goals of arousal and/or orgasm. Goals focus you on the future, taking you away from your experience of this moment. You can assist your sexual recovery by changing the definition of your activity to one that has no predetermined beginning or end.

6. Invite arousal, instead of forcing it

The natural arousal you were born with, that was enhanced by sexual hormones at puberty, has most likely been submerged for a long time. It may not surface just because you offer it a chance. Many invitations will permit natural arousal to emerge. Releasing the shame that covers it over will free you to rediscover your healthy sexual energy. This can't be forced. Only cross-wired or addictive sexual energy can be forced into your body, and driven to intense orgasm. *Inborn sexual energy doesn't respond to force or control.* It will venture out, given an invitation and a commitment to removing obstacles to its welcome.

7. View self-loving as an adventure in starting over

If you are like the vast majority of Americans, you have little sense of your healthy sexual energy. You aren't allowed to talk about how you stroked your body and noticed an erection, or other evidence of arousal; or how you stroked your genitals and had no arousal. Your friends aren't going to say, Oh, yes, I did that and it was nice. Sexual emerging isn't built into our culture, and so, unless you find a group of people who are also embarking on this exploration, you will be going it alone. It helps to view self-loving as an adventure, a lifetime of self-discovery.

BEGINNING

When you are ready to explore making love to yourself, I suggest the following ways to prepare. These are only suggestions to help you start on an adventure that has not been incorporated into our culture. As you begin your discoveries, your own preparation and approach will be best.

1. Find a time and place where you will not be interrupted and where you feel safe. Interruptions can evoke more shame than you can bear to flow through you, and they won't provide safety for the tender part of you that you are inviting out.

2. Begin by breathing and inviting yourself into your body. Notice what you feel as you prepare to explore. If fear and/or shame emerge, let them come, welcome them and breathe them through your body. These are the feelings you are setting out to divest from your sexuality.

3. When you are ready, begin touching yourself. Stroke your arms and face, your chest and stomach. Notice how you feel. When it is time, put your hand on your genitals. Allow time for emotions to emerge before continuing. Now explore your genitals. Notice their shape and texture. This is a wonderful part of your body, one you can invite back into your loving awareness, much as you did when you were a baby and first getting acquainted with your body parts.

4. If any cross-wired or addictive feelings come up, *stop*. The old kind of masturbation will reinforce itself, as will the new kind. Avoiding the old will allow faster access to the new.

5. Notice your arousal. See what allows it to start, and what you can do that brings it on more. See what feelings make you want to switch over to old ways, and let your body feel them. Don't worry if your arousal drops when fear and shame come up. Of course it will. Breathe. Notice the difference between emerging arousal and the old, intense kind that wanted orgasm.

6. From here on, your story is your own. I have heard many reports of people making love to themselves, and every experience is different.

7. It is time to stop when you are done. Only you will know when.

STORIES OF SELF-LOVING

I "assign" students in my Healthy Sexual Energy classes the task of healthy self-loving. Less than half do the assignment. It brings up too much shame and fear for those who have just begun their sexual recovery. I also bring it up as a topic for my men's therapy group, and my women's sexuality support group. These people have spent time removing shame from sexuality, and so find the assignment easier. The women I see, however, are less likely to do it than men.

Ben was able to go home from class and experiment with making love to himself. He had less shame than most people, and had been able to talk openly about sex in the men's therapy group prior to taking the class. He described how he lovingly touched his penis, had an erection and stayed in the present while feeling his arousal. Ben was in therapy because he was unable to commit to a relationship, always having two or more possible women without being able to choose one. Sex itself was not part of his addiction.

Everyone in the room froze when Ben said that he massaged his anus while rubbing his penis. It is forbidden to disclose this information, especially for men who are expected to consider anal stimulation a homosexual activity—something not accepted by our culture, and not within the scope of activities permissible for "real men." But as he spoke, the listeners in the room softened and energy began again to flow. As people went around the room describing their experience, two more men said they also rubbed their anuses for arousal.

Paul had been addicted to affairs through most of his long marriage. At the time he entered the men's group, he was still using pornography, as sex therapists had recommended. After he had given up masturbation and sex for six months, I coached him on sexual self-loving. He was fascinated by the idea, and went home to give it a try.

Paul found that in the beginning he didn't have an erection, and wanted to fantasize to get one. However, over the course of an hour, he found that arousal came from an unfamiliar place, and felt very different from the arousal that came from watching scenes of forbidden sex. He could sense the difference, as he experienced shame-free arousal for the first time. He described how he felt open and glowing for a few minutes, and then discovered that he was in sexual fantasy. When he could observe that, he stopped touching his body and waited until he could get back with himself. Then he resumed exploring.

I was touched by Paul's first experience of self-loving. His wife had feared he was hopeless and could never have a loving sexual relationship. At age fifty-seven, Paul was determined to eradicate the influence his mother had on him when she shamed him for just about everything. She hated his father for wanting sex. Paul heard them fight over it, and saw his father angrily return to his own room after being treated like a rapist. This constant input through his childhood, and his belief that he was a bad boy, resulted in sex being possible only when he was being "bad." His wife wouldn't be bad with him, and so he was stricken with an inability to become aroused when trying to have sex with her. Now he was proving his mother wrong as he lovingly caressed himself to arousal, and refused to get into the shame compartment where he had spent his entire sex life.

Richard began exploring self-loving when he realized he was addicted to his wife's sexual interest in him. He found it wonderfully freeing to sit in an outdoor hot tub and be with his sexual self. When he began, he had no goal of being sexual or of reaching orgasm. He was focused on being whole and separate, alone and yet with himself. His mood made it possible to be with himself sexually, as well.

Peter started the exercise, knowing he would talk about the results in the next men's group meeting. But he found that his shame crept up so fast each time he started that he was unable to continue. Instead, he focused on his shame and the desire to escape it by fantasizing about watching other people having sex. He wanted to watch a video, but knew that didn't qualify for the assignment. The lesson made him vividly aware of the reality of the shame compartment, no longer just a concept I had presented. He was able to begin looking at the shame he was trying to avoid with the use of pornography, and to trace it back to a shaming childhood. He had been heavily shamed for masturbating, and was told that God would punish him. The shame "took," but he continued to masturbate. He removed the feeling of shame by having sex with people in videos.

Larry didn't try to make love to himself. He couldn't imagine touching his genitals unless he were thoroughly aroused and he believed he had to have an orgasm to end the sexual feelings. He had intense shame about his sexuality. He had been unable to make love with his wife once he'd stopped drinking and gone into recovery for alcoholism. The alcohol had numbed him to the shame and permitted his cross-wired fantasies to arouse him. Now, with neither, he was left raw. Not only was he unable to become aroused, he also felt intense distress.

Sam's first contact with the idea of self-loving was in my Healthy Sexual Energy class. Months later, he entered therapy, and months after that he shyly told me about his first self-loving. In the beginning, the task had seemed overwhelming, and impossible. But in time, as he heard other men talk about it, he considered the idea and was finally able to try it. He began by touching himself for only a few minutes, and gradually increased the amount of time as he disengaged from his overlay of shame.

The women in the women's group were more reluctant to make love to themselves and tell the stories. Women typically are less interested in pornography and fantasizing about other lovers. Instead, they are more likely to depend on the approach of their mate to take them into the shame compartment. For women, the use of romance, tenderness and seduction are analogous to the use of pornography for men. Romance novels sell millions each year, attracting women by creating sexual arousal or diffuse sexual feelings by describing relating between men and women. The relationships may be abusive, and depend on relationship addiction, yet they are not often seen as pornographic. In fact, they are as much cross-wired arousers as pictures of sex scenes.

Jan has not been able to make love to herself. When she thought of trying it, she became immediately aroused. Because this arousal didn't serve the bonding with her mate, or her personal sexual-spiritual experience, she knew it was cross-wired. It felt desperate and hard rather than open and free. When she agreed with her body to forgo the exercise, the arousal dropped off. She could, of course, masturbate. When she does, she receives sexual recovery lessons. But this particular form of learning hasn't been available to her yet.

Margaret was able to stay present with herself when she tried the exercise until she reached the point of wanting an orgasm. Then she went into fantasy, knowing it was the only way to reach her climax. Years before she had read a book that taught her to use fantasy in order to have orgasms, and this had been her only way to accomplish it. She said that when she had been stimulating herself for a time, she felt the strong urge for orgasm, and at that point moved into cross-wired arousal.

When Margaret finished her explorations of self-loving, she got in her car to pick up her children from school. As she drove, she was washed with shame, sure that everyone around her could tell she had been sexual with herself. If she had masturbated in old ways, she would not have had this experience because she had been able to isolate her sexuality and stay in the shame compartment. By staying present, however, she forced herself to feel the shame attached to her sexuality. For Margaret, shame didn't show up while she was being sexual. Rather, she experienced it when thinking people knew what she was doing.

Deb told us that when she touched herself lovingly, she was surprised to find that she lubricated and her clitoris swelled. She enjoyed stimulating herself, really knowing what she was doing. As Deb told us about her experience, she said that she had to overcome self-hate in order to stay present for as long as she did. She was nude, which brought up hatred for her body. This one time, she was able to look at her legs and like them even though she considers them fat. She was able to know that her feelings of self-hate don't have to do with her body parts, but rather is a feeling common to many women. Our worth is defined by our sexual appeal to men, and so it is easy to hate the bodies we live in. Few of us qualify as adequate sex objects.

Deb lost her arousal when her self-hate took over again, and immediately went into cross-wired stimulation patterns because she didn't want to lose the arousal. She wanted to make it last. The only way to do so was to override her body's decision and make her arousal return.

Jennifer said she had been unable to try the exercise because she couldn't think of sex as something to do for herself. She said she grew up seeing women as men's playthings. Even learning to be orgasmic is accomplished in order to be adequate for men. The thought of trying the exercise brought up feelings of being bad for wanting sex. She is torn between the requirement of wanting sex because she is married, and the prohibition against being the kind of woman who wants sex. In this day of post-sexual revolution, we act as if these factors no longer affect our sexuality. In truth, we are all still affected by these centuries-old attitudes.

Chapter 10

Inviting Healthy Sexuality

I have prepared some guidelines as the two of you, together, create your own environment for further sexual healing. The first of these has to do with the perception of sex as the primary focus of the activity.

SEX IS ABOUT HAVING FEELINGS— NOT ABOUT HAVING SEX

I suggest that you change your entire perception of sex, no longer seeing it as an end in itself, or an occasional activity. Instead, we can understand that sex has tremendous overlays of shame from our culture and from particular childhoods. It carries with it all the societal implications, such as proving love, masculinity, femininity, prowess, attractiveness and worth. *Your associations must be stripped away before you can use sex in the way it was intended. You can do this by focusing on your feelings while engaging sexually.*

Early in our sexual recovery—Rex's and mine—I was bound by the rule that once I began sexual activity, I had to continue until we were "done." Yet, frequently, I lost my arousal before either of us had orgasm. I had learned prior to my sexual recovery how to keep my arousal going. I would tighten up my body, and direct my attention into my genitals. I would moved my body differently, or change position to enhance arousal. I would fantasize about sexual activities that were guaranteed to arouse me. It was a lot of work. It took me away from my partner. But I didn't stop.

When Rex and I agreed always to put feelings before rules about sex, I began to speak up when my arousal dropped. My "voices" said I was inadequate as a woman, I wasn't truly a sexual person and I was wronging him. Rex's voices said that he wasn't pleasing me sufficiently, that he wasn't attractive to me and that I didn't love him enough. As we spoke, we could see the absurdity, although guilt on both sides lingered for months. In two to three years it was eliminated. Then we discovered that our bodies knew what they were doing. We had made room for them to communicate to each other. As we respected this, we found that when one of us loses óur arousal the other does also. We don't know if the second loss is a response to the first, or if they are simultaneous. We guess they're simultaneous. When that happens, we go on with what we want to do next.

No Orgasm For A Time

It is difficult for most people, even after a moratorium, to return to sexual activity and forgo the old rules. I have found that giving up orgasm during an extended period allows new experiences that might otherwise take a long time to occur. By not having orgasms you won't be goal-directed in sex. There is no identifiable ending period and nothing to work toward. By our culture's definition, you won't "have sex." In time you will get to see that orgasm doesn't determine "having sex." Instead, touching each other and feeling sexual becomes real sex, regardless of what you do with the feelings.

One morning Rex and I were standing in our dressing area just before Rex left for work. For about five minutes we kissed, and found sexual energy flowing up in great sweeps. As he prepared to leave, I told him that I would like to have sex, even though I knew at the moment we couldn't. He smiled at me, and said, "We just did!"

After he left, I realized that my old programming told me we'd merely had a taste of what we really wanted. If I'd stayed in that place I would have felt deprived, and perhaps looked forward to the evening when we could "finish what we started." I may have blamed him for getting me ready for something I couldn't have. But when Rex reframed our delicious sexual exchange as complete in itself, my perception could change, too. It had been perfectly wonderful to feel the energy swirling through me. My body felt alive, and I lived fully in it— reminded again of my physical self by the sexual arousal. I felt lovingly bonded with Rex. As I reflected on these events, I could see the absurdity of thinking we hadn't had sex. If we had a moratorium on orgasms, I wouldn't have had that confusion.

Moving toward orgasm is the time that is most likely to elicit emotional abandonment of your partner, and a turning of your attention to building arousal. At such a time, there are two reasons we are likely to use the most powerful cross-wiring that brings on intense arousal: One is that orgasm requires intense sexual feelings, and if they don't come naturally then they must be coerced. The second is that orgasm is a tremendously vulnerable experience, and cross-wired thoughts can prevent the experience of intimacy, thus preventing fear. These two elements of sex can be separated from your work on other components, and can be added later when New Sex is more familiar and better understood.

No Goals

When we focus on what we should be doing next, we are not in the present. Being in the present is a component of intimacy, and so the moment we think about what we will be doing a minute from now we are not relating intimately with our lover. The truth is that our bodies can make all the decisions about sex—when we let them. Our bodies can communicate with each other about what should happen next, and do it without our ever thinking about it. We can *let* it happen rather than *make* it happen. That is the essence of inside-out sex.

Healthy Sex Is Not Urgent

The term "sexual desire" implies that sexual arousal automatically leads to more sexual activity. You "desire" something. *I invite you to take a new look at sexual arousal as being complete in itself whether acted on or not.*

Addictive sexuality is filled with urgency, needing more and more, until the orgasm ends the trance. But gently unfolding sexuality can come and go easily. If your partner's feelings come up, and your attention turns to them, your sexual energy can continue to be present with you. You don't have to turn it off, or "satisfy" it. Sexual feelings are a part of being human.

Our culture hasn't helped us to know about this. By its eroticizing us, and also prohibiting the natural unfolding of sexual energy, we've become overly reactive to cross-wired stimuli. If you find yourself avidly wanting to do more, then it is time to listen to your feelings. The belief that you can't stop, once the feelings come up, is due to cross-wiring, and will change as you invite a different kind of arousal. ***When your "desire" seems strong, stop, and see what happens next.*** Notice where the sexual feeling is in your body, and what happens when you pay attention to it. Notice what emotions come up when you don't continue to engage in sexual activity.

USING NO OUTSIDE–IN STIMULATORS

In the past you and your partner might have watched sexual videos together, or shared fantasies as a way to encourage sexual arousal. You probably thought about having sex earlier in the day or before you were intimate with your mate. You might have felt arousal, unbidden by the nature of your relating, and assumed that it was "desire" to have sex. You might have seen a sexual stimulus on television, in a mall, on the street or at work that elicited sexual feelings that seemed to require obtaining "satisfaction" with your mate.

All forms of stimulation, including vibrators, "sexy" cloth-ing, pornography, thoughts about what is coming next and looking at body parts to the exclusion of the whole person, will take you away from the present and into cross-wired sexual arousal. (There may be a time when you want to introduce these cross-wirings deliberately so that you can heal from them, but now is not that time.) ***Intimate sex comes from the inside out, and will be inhibited by arousal stimulated from the outside in.***

RELINQUISHING *ALL* SEXUAL STEREOTYPES

Our culture has taught us that our intellect is the only valuable part of us—what we think is what we are. When this view is superimposed on sex, or on any other spiritual facet, those areas of our life become stopped up and no longer spiritual. From our training, we think we must maintain erections, we must look a certain way to stimulate our lovers, we must have sex a certain number of times a week and we must include certain activities to qualify as good lovers. We see sex as embarrassing, and the object of jokes, something to be hidden and never discussed.

We must relinquish all our stereotypes about sex, if we are to find out what lies underneath—the truth about our sexuality. The old views of sex prevent us from finding out what it really is. And we can find out by questioning everything—absolutely everything about our old views.

In my own questioning I had to consider that it was possible to have more than one lover. I opened myself to this possibility at the time I was getting to know Rex, and for a few weeks it seemed to be possible to have no jealousy about his other lover, and to feel no guilt about mine. We were open and honest about everything with everyone, which seemed to make the difference. We thought that deception was the culprit, and by eliminating that, we made it possible to have more than one lover. But in only a few weeks Rex and I had bonded into a monogamous marriage—with no conscious decision to do so, and almost against our will. ***By letting go of stereotypical ideas about sexual relationships, and opening ourselves up to the truth, we found that monogamy was natural to us.***

Other commonly accepted notions to question include:

1. We have a sex drive.

2. It is natural to be attracted to "sexy" people.

3. We must express our sexual selves by having sex.

4. Married, or otherwise coupled, people have to have sex.

5. Sexual feelings are "desire" for sex rather than just sexual feelings.

6. Something bad will happen if we are aroused for a long time, or with high intensity, if we don't have an orgasm.

7. People have different "sex drives."

8. Jealousy is always unhealthy.

9. Once we begin sex, we can't stop until we're "done."

10. If one partner loses arousal, the other is doing something wrong.

11. There is such a thing as a "good lover."

12. Fat people or old people aren't as sexual as thin or young people.

13. Menstruation is a bad time to have sex.

14. Something is wrong with us if we decide to have sex and fail to experience arousal.

15. Losing an erection means a man is a failure, or he isn't a "real man" or a good lover.

16. Having rapid orgasms or no orgasms or delayed orgasms is cause for shame.

Continue the list with items that influence your attitudes that interfere with loving, bonding sex.

STEPS TO INVITING SEXUAL EXPRESSION

Now that you and your partner have decided it is time to be sexual, you might imagine what it would have been like if you were around twelve or thirteen, and didn't know very much yet. How would you begin? Would you ask if you could look at breasts and vulva, penis and testicles?

If you were innocent children in a healthy culture, the tasks would be easy and you could learn what you needed to know quickly and efficiently. But that isn't the case now. You were damaged both by our culture and your childhood, and so you have to confront each erroneous message as it comes up. This is how you can get back to what is natural. ***It means going very slowly, adding one sexual activity at a time, letting yourself express all the feelings that emerge.***

There is no particular order to the introduction of sexual activities. Each of you can think about the way you might get started sexually, and see what distress it brings up. Then begin with that. For example, when Monty and Trina decided to end their sexual moratorium, Monty was terrified by even the thought of getting started. He had just discovered that he was a sex addict, and was eagerly undoing both his addictive use of sex, and his cross-wiring. He was afraid that if he became sexual with Trina he would become addicted all over again.

Monty's fear subsided when he and Trina came in for a session to learn how to approach sex. When he discovered that they weren't just going back to the old ways in which they had been sexual, he was tremendously relieved. He could see that he still had control over his sex life, and that if he found himself feeling addictive or wanting to use cross-wired activities, he could say no and stop. Trina supported this because she knew that she must always stop when she didn't feel sex was right, and so she understood he had the same need. She also didn't want him to be sexual when he wasn't comfortable because then they could not be intimate.

Eager to get started, they began to examine sexual activities to find out what feelings were likely to emerge. Both realized that for Trina, having her breasts touched was going to bring up distress because she had expressed discomfort in the past. They had never talked about it before the moratorium, but both were aware that she often felt fear and dread when Monty touched her there. Now they could see that this fear needed to be introduced consciously and deliberately so she could have the feelings, and remove them from her body. They could see the need for attention to her breasts, with no further sexual activity, while Trina took the opportunity to feel her fear so she could release it.

Monty knew that for him, intercourse would be a time of the most intense feelings. Needing to do it "right" would prevent him from staying in the present with Trina. Therefore he knew he wanted to have many sexual encounters and to learn how to have the feelings as they emerged—all before he was ready to try intercourse.

Some couples find being naked together fearful, while others are comfortable without clothes. Some find kissing natural and non-threatening, while for others it is loaded with shame from the past or brings up fear of intimacy. Take a look at the following list of sexual activities and add all your own items. Notice your cross-wired reactions when you imagine them. Note what non-sexual feelings come up.

This is a skeletal list of specific activities that often go on during sex.

✦ nudity

✦ looking at the other's body

✦ having your body looked at

✦ looking deeply into each other's eyes

✦ kissing in a way that invites sexual arousal

✦ stroking skin, non-erogenous areas of body

✦ having skin stroked, non-erogenous areas of body

✦ stroking buttocks, inner thighs and other areas you consider erogenous

✦ having buttocks, inner thighs and other areas you consider erogenous stroked.

✦ touching of nipples by partner

✦ touching of nipples by self with partner present

✦ touching of scrotum by partner

✦ touching of scrotum by self with partner present

✦ touching of vulva (including vagina, clitoris and labia) by self with partner present

✦ touching of vulva (including vagina, clitoris and labia) by partner

✦ oral stimulation of vulva

✦ oral stimulation of penis

✦ oral stimulation of scrotum and testicles

✦ touching of your anus by partner

✦ touching partner's anus

✦ touching your anus with partner present

✦ putting your penis at the opening of partner's vagina

✦ having a penis placed at the opening of your vagina

✦ pushing penis into a vagina

✦ having a penis pushed into your vagina

✦ slow movement during intercourse

✦ rapid movement during intercourse

✦ hard contact between bodies when penis has fully penetrated into vagina

✦ placing head of penis on partner's anus

✦ having partner's penis placed on your anus

✦ pushing penis into partner's anus

✦ having penis pushed into your anus

✦ moving penis in and out of partner's anus

✦ penis moving in and out of your anus

✦ stimulating partner's anus with your mouth

✦ partner stimulating your anus with mouth

I have named some common forms of sexual stimulation that can be part of healthy sexual expression. (These same events can also be cross-wired—something you can determine as you explore.) The list does not imply that you should examine all items. Some may not be relevant to you, others will. In addition, you may have your own activities that you can examine to learn about your feelings, and to see if you are cross-wired in ways you may want to examine. Cross-wired arousal does not enhance intimacy with yourself or your mate, and so identifying it is one object of this approach to sexual re-learning.

There are some sexual activities that are always cross-wired. Being tied up is re-abuse, even if it is done safely and brings arousal. It is not something you should feel shame about—either wanting to tie someone up or being tied up—but is something to examine for the feelings you may want to relinquish from the past.

Pretending as if you are other people, or in another situation, are examples of activities that may be added to the list to be addressed, in order to elicit feelings. However, they aren't among the activities of healthy sex.

Imagining you are some place other than in bed with your mate takes you away from the present, which is incompatible with intimacy. While there is nothing "wrong" with this, it will deprive you of the kind of healthy sexual interaction that is more fulfilling.

How Much Fear?

As you read the list above, notice which items bring up fear, shame or other negative feelings. This will give you an idea of the order in which you might introduce activities into your sex life. I suggest you begin with those that elicit less feeling, and set aside those with more for special attention.

Please don't push too fast. While our culture tells us that sex is natural and easy, this is absolutely not true. We are programmed to inhibit our fears of sex and sexual shame so that we can function in spite of them. Now you will be inviting shame, fear, anger and other feelings. This is a major task when engaging in our most vulnerable activity. Please respect yourself and your right to go as slowly as you need, even if your partner seems ready to go much faster.

Invite Arousal, Don't Force It

Don't be surprised if sexual arousal fails to appear. We are so accustomed to responding to the cross-wired arousal our culture has conditioned in us that when we innocently wait for something to emerge from the inside-out, there isn't much room for it to do so. It is a different kind of sexual experience, one to be invited, not ordered, to emerge. We know how to order it out—any number of provocative stimuli from the outside will do it.

Not ordering it out is new. Waiting for it to appear isn't consistent with any images the media present, or that we garner in "locker room" talk, or in the bedroom. Sometimes people go for weeks or months without much sexual feeling. This is fine. You are making room for a different kind of sexuality. The old sexuality gets to die first.

How Much Cross-Wired Arousal?

Now examine the items according to how much sexual arousal you feel as you think of the activity. Chances are that all the arousal you experience is cross-wired. Make note of it so you can explore more later, as your sexual contact gets underway. One of the tasks of sexual recovery is identifying the difference between body sensations of cross-wired sexuality and the healthy, unfolding kind of arousal. Inviting consciousness of them can help when you ask yourself, your feelings and your body the question, "What happened earlier in my life to create this association between sex and something that isn't inherently sexual?"

When you feel cross-wired arousal come up, it is a good time to stop and begin questioning: How did it get here? What happened that created this method of achieving sexual arousal? What would happen if you didn't have this cross-wiring?

Barry found that he could count on becoming aroused if his partner looked hurt and if her body was positioned in a way that revealed the profile of her breasts and a turning away from him. He positioned her body during sexual activity to enhance his arousal, and talked to her in ways that elicited his favored facial expressions. If he didn't do this, he didn't get aroused, which frightened him. He didn't understand that he didn't have access to his healthy sexuality, and so was stuck with the cross-wired kind. In time he was able to tolerate his fear of not being aroused when wanting to be sexual, and having to wait for a different kind of experience. When he did gain access to healthy sexuality, he was greatly relieved to find that I had told him the truth, that indeed, something better was possible.

BEGINNING

Set aside time with your partner to be together when you won't be disturbed. Go to a room in the house where you feel safe. This may or may not be your bedroom. For those who were violated in their bedrooms as children, the associations may not be of safety. As you sit down together to decide how to get started, begin with a check-in. How are you feeling about yourself? How has your day gone? What are your feelings toward your mate? Do you really want to work on sexuality right now? Resolve any unfinished business before entering this more risky area of relating. If you can't, then perhaps this isn't time for sex.

Feeling Horny Isn't the Time to Have Sex

Choose a time to explore when you aren't feeling sexual. If you begin when you feel "horny," or aroused, the drug effect of the arousal can prevent fear and shame. If you prevent these feelings, then you postpone removing them from your sexuality. As you make room for sexual feelings of a different nature than what you previously accepted as "normal," you will be best served if you don't start with old sexual feelings.

Breathe, Breathe, Breathe

Breathe. This is scary work. Anyone in our culture doing these exercises can expect to feel fear and shame. Breathing can assist you in staying conscious and within your body. If it doesn't work, then you may not be in a place to begin this project. Please respect your defenses. If they are operating, it may not yet be time to push on. Instead, find out what they are defending you from and take a look at *that*. For example, if you were the object of a parent's sexual interest, whether it was expressed sexually or not, you might find fear coming up over the idea of conscious sex even before you get started. Your fear is telling you that this is the place you can start to take a look at yourself.

Telling the Truth

Tell the whole truth. If you withhold any information about your feelings, you are deceiving your mate, and making intimacy impossible. This means if you don't want to be sexual when she or he expresses an interest, you have to say so. If you go ahead because it seems like no big deal, you are depriving both of you from knowing what is possible.

If your cross-wiring comes up suddenly, perhaps as a way to create distance or maintain a flagging arousal, you will have to stop sex and tell your partner. This can be painful if you are thinking of another lover or another time. Yet to withhold the information will surely end your intimacy. When you cut yourself off from your mate, he or she knows, although perhaps not consciously. We all know everything that is going on, and we react to it even if we can't articulate it. Each time we withhold from our mate, she or he is reacting to that withholding. Then we react to the reaction. By this time it becomes quite difficult to figure out what has gone on.

I used to think I could hide my mood and feelings from clients, and put on a helping therapist's face, whether or not that reflected the way I felt. But one day, a client gave me information about myself that matched my cross-wiring, and which I hadn't been aware of revealing. This jolted me into knowing that I wasn't hiding anything, and so I may as well live true to my experience. With trepidation I began doing so, and met with many surprised and shocked reactions. Some clients were angry with me when I yawned and looked bored. But most of them were, in the long run, grateful to have a therapist who would be real with them as they struggled to be real in the world. Therapy became much easier because the act had been a lot of work.

Containing Your Feelings

Bringing up feelings is only the first part. The question is, now that they are here, what do you do with them? Here is where the container, described in Chapter 7, can be useful. As each feeling emerges, the feeling takes priority over sexual activity. Letting the feelings tell the story of abuses from the past can encourage sexual healing.

Feelings that occur in the context of a relationship are intense, as you already know. When you focus specifically on sexual issues, feelings are likely to become even more intense. Sexual shame, jealousy, fear and anger are the just the start of what is possible. You may find that you need a therapist's help while exploring what comes up during your adventure.

Among the more challenging feelings are your reactions to your mate's cross-wiring. If he desires a body that is thinner and different from yours, it is natural for you to react with anger and hurt. Most couples stop at this place, and try to cope with the feelings. This is done by lying about the cross-wiring, hiding it and going into silent fantasy instead, while the mate pretends the feelings aren't there even while intuiting them.

If she desires a lover who is more sensitive to her body, but doesn't want to hurt her partner's feelings by speaking, her mate will be violated by her dishonesty.

I invite you to take the honest route. It may seem more painful, but it is the only way out of the trap of sexual distortion that is universal in our culture. On the journey, stay with each other's painful feelings. As you see that your mate's cross-wiring is the result of childhood abuses, it becomes increasingly possible to tolerate it while she or he goes to work on it. Rex says that we are constantly molting—bringing up, pulling out, feeling, dropping and replacing old patterns from the past.

Notice Your Expectations

As soon as you decide to be "sexual," your first set of expectations, learned long ago, will show up. For example, when Rex and I began our discovery, each time we got out of the shower and went to the bed, I had an awkward feeling about what "should" happen next. I couldn't figure out how to lie down on the bed "right," or how to touch him. My stereotypical notion told me that I should lie down and he should proceed to "make love" to me. And I shouldn't do anything in the beginning because I am the woman and I believe the man needs to be in control. If I abandoned these ideas, then I didn't know what to do!

I immediately focused on sexual arousal, and thought about all the old ways of forcing it to appear. When I dismissed them, I was left confused, as if I'd never had sex before. Now, six years later I find myself feeling confused occasionally about what to expect. But I can laugh, and guess that Rex is probably having the same feeling. We exaggerate it by acting it out, grimacing and dramatically trying different things, dismissing each one as the next comes up. Soon we are hugging. enjoying being together, and not expecting anything. If arousal comes, we will build on it and enjoy it. If other ways of being together happen, then we know that is right for us.

INVENTING YOUR OWN EXPLORATION

From here on, your exploration will be all your own. Every couple will have a different adventure because we each begin with our own fears and cross-wiring. If you can accept your feelings as your own (perhaps triggered by the other person), take all the time you need (minutes, hours, days, weeks, months and years), start only when it feels sufficiently safe, and stop when you have had enough, you will then embark on an adventure and achieve a great education. Go for it! I would love to hear your story if you would like to drop me a note.

Chapter 11

What Is Healthy Sexuality?

I t is joyful to couples when both partners agree to have or not to have sex. As bodies and souls are tuned in to each other, it no longer makes sense to want to have sex with someone who isn't present or who isn't interested. As it becomes clear that sex isn't a drive or an appetite, and that it isn't a need that belongs to the individual irrespective of the partnership, it begins to feel ridiculous to imagine that one could want to be sexual when the other one doesn't.

DANIEL AND EMILY

Daniel wanted sex with Emily constantly, and felt bereft when she wanted "her nights" and "his nights." On hers, they didn't have sex, and on his she gave in. But even on his nights, she didn't want to, because she never had a chance to develop an interest. Dutifully, she couldn't say no.

After a few therapy sessions with Daniel, examining his feelings about sex with an unwilling partner, he began to realize how bad it felt to beg for sex, to ask for favors and to plan how to get her to say yes. He could see that he was damaging his self-esteem by putting so much emphasis on his wife's consent. Soon he pulled back, and really asked himself if he wanted to have sex under those circumstances. He chose not to. This was the beginning of his freedom from compulsive sex. His feelings of self-caring grew quickly as he no longer begged for crumbs or settled for "sexual satisfaction" given from a place of long-suffering duty.

Daniel worked quickly on his addiction, open to seeing how painful it was to him to be engaged sexually by himself while with her. As his "addict" diminished, he came to have a self-respecting use of sexuality.

Daniel and Emily described a recent experience of sex—well on the road to healthy, spiritual sexuality. It began when Daniel became aware that he was feeling warmly sexual, and told Emily. She said she was, too. This was so different from his usual request for sex and her required answer that neither of them knew what to do next!

They were lying down. Emily had her back cuddled up against Daniel's front. He found his erection growing. She suggested that he rub against her and have an orgasm, since she was not feeling interested in intercourse. This was one of their long-standing solutions to his greater interest in sex.

Emily felt comfortable as Daniel rocked her body, but she didn't become aroused. Daniel described how he had to rub to keep his erection up, and at one point it diminished. He remembered his conversations with me about one-sided sex leaving him feeling empty, and he respected his penis's message. His addict tried once more to get the sexual feelings back by rubbing against Emily, but the arousal that came didn't seem worth the effort. Daniel's addict was dying.

As Daniel, erectionless, snuggled up to Emily's back, she rolled over to face him. I asked her what was happening when she did that, and she began to describe the deeply spiritual place she had been in. I can't recapture her images, but my sense as she spoke was a place that was entirely safe, self-loving and wise. From this place her body decided to roll over. She had no conscious thought and made no conscious decision about it, she just did it.

As they faced each other, Daniel asked if Emily was suggesting sex. She said she wanted to lie together without moving. They did.

Daniel tried to describe his knowing that lying together without motion, wrapping themselves around each other, was far more loving than the sex they'd had in the past. They gazed into each other's eyes, melting into one another.

Then gradually they found themselves aroused sexually, and moving gracefully into sexual activity. Intercourse only extended the physical marriage they were already experiencing. Both were unable to tell me what they did sexually. They couldn't remember. *This made sense to me because when sex comes from a spiritual place, the acts "performed" are not the center of the experience. They are only the form sexual marrying takes.* The two of them were, however, able to talk about what they didn't do. Daniel said there was no order to their activities, and he didn't think in terms of what he should do next to see if it would arouse Emily. Sex was not a "job" to see if he could "please" his wife so she would "meet his needs."

Emily said that for her, nothing about this sex resembled the way it had been for years. She did note that when she and Daniel first hugged as teenagers, she'd felt the warmth and openness of his body. She was deeply grateful that his "addict" was dying so that she could have that long-ago experience, only now with the richness of their years together.

I watched their faces and bodies as they told me the story. As they looked at each other, and touched occasionally, I could see the bonding energy moving between them. I knew this was the energy that allowed them to join sexually in a way that surpasses description. My usual words as a therapist were so inadequate that I said little. Their education about spiritually bonding sex was so complete that my words, along with theirs, could only fall short.

MAGGIE AND RICHARD

Maggie walked into the couples group with Richard beaming behind her. They looked like little kids with a secret, waiting to share it. These two had been married for five years, after their first marriages ended in divorce. Both were recovering sex addicts, learning to identify when their addictions took over and prevented them from loving with intimacy.

They began by telling us they'd had the most unusual sex together that either one had ever known, and wondered if they had stumbled onto the healthy kind. As they described it, I believed they had.

Richard said that he hadn't expected to have sex that night because Maggie had come home from the women's Sunday gathering. He knew from experience that she didn't want sex after a day of talking about feelings. Maggie assumed the same. They had gone to bed to sleep, and found themselves holding each other tenderly. Both of them had difficulty piecing together the order of events because their activities had been so different from their usual exchange. Richard found himself lying on top of Maggie, feeling the warmth of her beneath him. She stroked his back in a way that made him feel totally loved and accepted, and brought tears to his eyes. He ran his hands over her body with no desire to arouse her sexually, but just to make contact with her.

"Then she was lying on top of me, and I was stroking her. The next thing I realized, we were making love. We were aroused. But it wasn't like any arousal I've known. It was so complete, like every bit of both our bodies were making love with every other bit. It seemed like it could go on forever. There was no beginning, middle or end. As I look back on it, I didn't define it as making love. I never thought that we would continue what we were doing. It seemed like it was happening just for this moment. It wasn't until afterward that we realized that we had just had sex. I could hardly wait to get here to talk about it."

Maggie continued, "I felt so loving toward Richard. I felt respected by his not pushing for sex, as he so often does. Instead of fighting against him, I felt invited to join him. These words don't really describe what happened, but this is as close as I can get.

"He touched me in ways that didn't feel sexual, they felt loving and kind, even though he touched me in the same places that he always does when he wants sex. His intention felt totally different. I didn't think we would have sex either. I didn't notice when my feelings became sexual. I hardly noticed when we were having intercourse. It all felt like the same thing we were doing—the non-sexual part and then the sexual part. My attention was more on the feeling of filling out my skin, and blending with Richard's. We kind of blended together, squishy and formless. We never asked what we were going to do next, or how to have an orgasm, or if we even wanted orgasms. *The facts of sex lost their importance.*"

The group was astonished, and hopeful. But one man said he was frustrated by the fact that he couldn't make that happen. It seemed that you had to wait for it. He didn't want to give up the expectation that he would ever have sex again in order to make room for the kind of experience that Richard and Maggie described. To him it was paradoxical to give up sexual goals in order to meet his goal of healthy sex.

Maggie and Richard completed their story by telling us that they hadn't been able to do this again. Richard wanted to try again the next day, but Maggie felt pressured and said no. Richard was angry and wanted to blame her for not having more healthy sex, and once again they were in their old patterns that prevented them from letting sex emerge. But now they know what it is like and will get there more quickly next time.

TRINA AND MONTY

Monty looked bright and full when he arrived for the weekly meeting of the men's group. After waiting until other men had a chance to discharge some of their feelings, he told about having intercourse for the first time in nine months. He and Trina had decided four months earlier to abandon the sexual moratorium, but his fear of conscious sex prevented them from exploring much further than holding each other with no clothes on.

Over a period of two hours they touched and kissed, became aroused, lost arousal and became aroused again. When feelings came up for one, they stopped sexual activity and focused on the feeling.

When they became ready to try intercourse, Monty reached for the lubricant. Trina felt a welling of rage. She told him she was angry, and asked if he could put on his psychic armour. He put down the Astroglide™ and sat back, looking at her. Trina, after a few deep breaths, let her anger out. She went back into memory—the years when Monty would reach for the lubricant immediately, not willing to wait for the natural body lubrication that comes with arousal. During those years she had sex only to satisfy his addictive desires, and so of course wanted the lubricant too. She didn't have to think about become aroused sufficiently to produce her own, and so it was a useful tool to meet her obligation. In the past she didn't feel the anger because she was playing out her part in the agreed relationship—she needed him to want her sexually to assure her place in the marriage, even though she felt used in the process. In truth, both were using each other.

Monty sat still, letting her anger wash over him. He remembered the countless times he reached for lubricant, tense and eager for his orgasm. Now he could see his wife, understanding the distress this had caused her. He knew he wasn't the same person. Now his reaching for the lubricant was only habit, resulting from his lack of understanding that she could provide enough when both of their bodies were truly ready for intercourse.

In a few minutes Trina was crying, reaching out to touch her husband. Once her anger had been discharged she was able to see who he is now and appreciate the difference in their loving. They held each other, reflecting over the emotional work that allowed this new way of being intimate. Both felt that sex was secondary to the power of their emotional exchange. But they also were interested in intercourse for one of its vital functions—pregnancy. Their daughter was almost three, and they wanted a second child soon. Looking into each other's eyes, they decided to continue sexual activity, and had their first intercourse. Monte's ejaculation was very important, but now for reasons entirely different from his addictive needs.

REX AND ANNE

I am ending this chapter with two descriptions of my own experience of sex. As with the couples described above, words were hard to find.

A Loving Vacation

When Rex and I were on a relaxing vacation we had sex, and afterward I wrote about it. The writing, reading it back to him and reading it now, months later, allowed me to capture the special lessons. When we just go on with our lives, it is hard to remember the specifics of sex. I think this is true for "old sex" because sex isn't talked about in our culture, and because the shame compartment isolates us from the rest of our lives, and for new sex because it is of a different order of experience and we don't have language that matches. This experience was recorded minutes later, and so is more available to see. As I re-read it, I saw how much emphasis I had placed on the remaining patterns inhibiting us. Yet my images, feelings and kinesthetic sense of the sex was that it was vastly spiritual. The new, bonding nature of our sex doesn't lend itself to description, while the old patterns are easier to see. I include this description to make the point that even sex fraught with old obstacles can also be the healthy variety. It was "perfect" even while influenced by the past.

I wrote:

On a tropical vacation we spend ten lazy days putting out little more energy than finding a place to eat each evening. One morning I hear him call out to me as he awakes. I climb back in bed, snuggling as we do almost every morning. I feel his skin, open and molding, receiving me and giving back.

We notice that our bodies are saying something about sex. I feel a hesitation because I have been uncovering more about my incestuous past, and the fear I felt then is surfacing. But our bodies are speaking clearly. I don't feel aroused exactly, rather a feeling of forward motion, of "yes," of moving toward, speaks to me. I know if I override it, I will feel narrowed down, lessened and my day will be smaller. This is not just about sex, but about following intuitive knowing of what is right for me.

I let my "voices" express my hesitation, and they say this: "I don't want to have an orgasm. So I'm not going to. If I want to have one I'll do it later if I feel like it. I'm not going to have an orgasm. I'm not"

As my voices speak and I see that Rex is still with me, I relax into a feeling that is both open and sexual. We bring our bodies together to see what they want to do.

With touch and intercourse we feel our electric arousal become intense, vibrating through our bodies. For a minute or so Rex's penis becomes smaller but the electric energy is still there, alerting us that we aren't finished just because his penis isn't full-size. Soon it is fully hard, and we continue. We look at each other, expanding into each other with the welcomed arousal that floods through our bodies. Minutes or perhaps hours pass—time ceases to be part of our knowing.

Then my body speaks to me about its desire to have an orgasm. The electricity around my clitoris feels the way it does just before orgasm, and my fear begins to grow. In moments, the electricity is gone. Rex asks if I have left, and I realize I have. As we are acknowledging that the electricity is gone, I ask if his penis is going down. I needn't ask because we both know this is, of course, happening.

I look into his face, seeing his love of us, his continuing joy in being together.

I hear distant voices saying that he is being a considerate man to let me stop sex when I want to, that I should appreciate that about him. But I know these voices aren't speaking the truth. I can see that he can do nothing else but lose his arousal when mine goes. Our bodies communicate, and his knows that if he were to continue wanting sex it would be a violation of me, of us and of him. It would be like rape, or wanting to rape, if his body wanted to have sex with a body that no longer wanted to. Now that he respects his body, he can hear the message that sex is over for now.

I see all of this in his face and I feel more loved than I have imagined possible. This is not love that is felt by him and expressed toward me. It is Rex being true to himself while with me. As he loves himself, I also am loved, and our relationship is created anew.

We lie together, basking in the warm, open face we see before us, and squish our bodies together. Our fat folds into each other's, bonding and re-bonding us.

Then the closeness is frightening for him. He says something seemingly innocent about the coming day and I feel isolated and cut off. I check to see if my fears are speaking up again and get a negative reply. Before I have finished checking, he says he can see he wanted distance from this intensity. His unconscious chose a communication that was sure to get me to pull back so he wouldn't have to do it himself. Instead, it would look as if I was the one with the intrusive patterns. Again we smile, letting our "voices" have their chance to be heard, respecting the childhood experiences they believe are still true today, knowing they are giving us further information about fears we still need to work through.

Rex and I find sex to be a confusing, curious, always different experience, of a different order than either of us knew during our addictive, cross-wired days. In my attempts to put our experience into words I wrote the following as part of a piece for an anthology on sex and alcohol.

Healthy Sex

We arise early today because the sun is shining in our window, enticing us awake on our day off. As we stand at the end of our bed after pulling the covers into place, I see myself reflected in his adorable, fresh, childlike face surrounded by gray hair. He looks like how I feel. We hug, and I am aware of the bulge of my stomach pressed against his, the soft, friendliness of bodies long acquainted, each fold accustomed to the fit.

As my breasts and vulva ignite with sexual energy, I feel his penis growing against me. With the morning open before us, we don't have to ponder the decision our bodies are making. We can allow them to take over.

We take our sexual hum to the shower, soaping ourselves and each other, touching our plump roundness. With twenty-five more pounds than when I was age thirty, I adore my body. Each square inch of both of us is the flesh we get to love each other in.

After we wash and scrub each other's backs with a loofa, we dry ourselves and return to bed to see what will happen next. Giggling like kids, we get on the bed. Sitting, we pat and stroke until the next thing to do becomes clear. Rex lies down and I lie on top of him. He touches my breasts, creating waves of sexual arousal that fill my chest and stream down through my pelvis. I put his penis at the opening of my vagina. His penis is about a third erect, quickly filling the rest of the way up as I hold it snugly against my waiting vagina. His penis hears my vulva, as they talk together to decide what we are to do next. If one doesn't want to continue, then neither of them does. They decide that inter-course is very desirable, and prepare by filling up with blood. They talk back and forth as both offer lubrication for a gentle entry. As his penis slides in, a wave of sparkling exuberance floods up my body and out, all over Rex. His floods all over me, too.

I move up and down to create friction to increase the swirling, electric arousal. Each cell in my vagina vibrates really fast, and the energy flows in different patterns within me and between us. We laugh again as our bodies swell and mold to each other. I stare into his eyes, drawing him into me as I watch his skin change and his breath expand. As we move and move, we feel our bodies approach orgasm, and then drop back, in unison. It isn't time to be finished, we want more.

I see that we have rolled over, and he is on top now, moving, and I have put my legs down to feel the pull on my clitoris, and the pressure of his legs moving against my inner thighs. All soft and plump, I feel formless and weightless, watching his muscles flex and release with each motion. I think we have been doing this for a very long time, but I'm not sure because I didn't look at the clock.

Then the arousal is gone. I startle slightly as I see that intercourse is over. As I look at Rex to tell him, he smiles at me. "My penis is going down," he says softly. "And your arousal is gone, isn't it?"

"Yes!" I tell him, still amazed that our bodies are able to decide these things, communicate to each other, and respond accordingly. Sometimes we can figure out why they have decided to take a certain course. Orgasms feel consistent with our stereotypical views of how sex should go, so that makes sense. But other times, like now, when we have plenty of time, we are loving each other and no incest memories are arising to interfere, it doesn't make much sense to our brains. But our bodies understand what we don't. We know that if we force arousal to continue, we lose each other, sometimes for hours. Instead, we embrace, smiling, stroking and feeling each other's plumpness.

Returning to the shower, we wash our juicy bodies, and our conversation turns to the day before us.

Appendix 1

REQUEST FOR INFORMATION TO BE USED IN FUTURE BOOK
From Generation to Generation: Learning About Adults Who Are Sexual With Children

As I work with people who have sexual problems, and see that shame is the primary culprit preventing people from discovering healthy sexuality, I have come to see the need to understand the role of the adult who is sexual with children. The kind of emotional work recommended in this book will change our culture as more and more of us work through the abuses of our sexuality. We will lift the shame and emerge out from under it as we really are, no longer subscribing to our culture's distortions of sexuality. But *in order to truly address cultural sexual shame, the person who was or is sexual with children, or who even thinks about doing so, must have an opportunity to recover too.* Our culture, at present, does not allow this.

I AM WRITING A BOOK

I am writing a book about the plight of the "adult who is sexual with children" (ASC). The purpose of the book is to take the shame off ASC's, and to educate the public about the culturally-supported nature of these acts. I know from my work with survivors, and with sex addicts, that many many adults have been sexual with young people. Some keep it a closely guarded secret, while others repress the memory to avoid shame. We are beginning to see the survivors as a cultural phenomena—now we must also see the ASC as a product of our culture.

I created the questionnaire at the end of this appendix so that people can anonymously provide information to be used in the book.

WILL YOU HELP?

I would like to request your help with collecting information about adults who have been sexual with young people, or who have had sexualized relationships without sex. Studies have not been done because those who might provide information to a scientist cannot do so without risk. The shame is intense, and the researcher may be required to make a report to child protective services if the behavior is still going on. By asking for anonymous information from those of you who have read this book, I can learn from you and pass the information on.

WHO ARE THE PEOPLE WHO ARE SEXUAL WITH CHILDREN?

In the past I believed people who were sexual with children had to be cruel and violent, with no concern for the needs of the innocent child. However, as I worked with more and more incest victims in my practice as a licensed psychologist, and as I learned about my own experience with incest, I gradually realized these stereotypes were untrue. In fact, most people who are sexual with children are quite passive, and may even be gentle people who seem unable to hurt a child. My own father was a highly respected professional. As I heard more and more stories about perfectly "normal" parents being sexual with their children I became curious about what was going on with them. How could they do things that violated society's and their values? What were they thinking and feeling when they were sexual? How did they handle the tremendous guilt that must accompany such acts?

In the beginning of my own recovery from incest I was bound by the stereotype of global badness, and so I couldn't believe my "nice" father had actually been sexual with me. I had to see him as an ordinary person, a victim of our culture and his childhood, before I could believe my emerging memories. I was able to learn from my experience as a psychologist. I was working with many incest victims whose lives were devastated by sexual abuse, and I would hear over and over how their parents or other relatives couldn't have done such things. After many times I began to believe that most of those involved in incest are parenting their children in ways they had been parented (typical people leading typical lives). They were unable to perceive the damage done to them, unable to see how they were passing it on to their own children. In short, once I realized this, I could view my own father in perspective. He was an emotionally isolated person who had a very good social image. He was successful in his career and respected by hundreds of people. I could know all of this was true, and at the same time comprehend that he had been sexual with me when I was a young child, and that, when I was older, even an adult, he crossed physical and sexual boundaries.

Mine was not an isolated case. *When we can believe that a minimum of one out of five of us was sexually violated in childhood, we can see this is not the exception in our culture, it is the norm.* Actually we were all violated, without our awareness, and usually without awareness of the adult who shamed and controlled our sexuality. We saw our elders express their discomfort in nonverbal ways, passing sexual shame from generation to generation, as we now pass it on to those who follow us.

ADULTS WHO ARE SEXUAL WITH CHILDREN MUST BE ABLE TO RECOVER

As it is now, survivors of sexual abuse are allowed to heal their wounds. Talk shows and therapist conferences focus vast amounts of energy on this recently visible area of pain. But the person who was sexual with a child is seen as horrible, one who deserves to be ostracized from society.

It is becoming understood by mental health professionals and the general public that sexual abuse is a generation to generation phenomenon. This means that those who were sexually abused are more likely to be sexual with the next generation. The implication of this fact is that many of the people in therapy for the effects of abuses done to them are keeping secrets about the behaviors they themselves have done. This secrecy is supported by therapists who blame the abuser. When the client hears blaming, he or she knows the therapist could hold the same attitude toward their behavior as well. While honesty is necessary when healing from sexual abuses, those who have secretly violated the sexuality of children must hold something back. This has to change before our culture can offer a truly healing medium for our sexuality. The purpose of my book, to be called *From Generation to Generation: Learning About Adults Who Are Sexual With Children*, is to alert our culture about the need to embrace all sexual shame, and all sexual distortions. The ASC isn't a bad person. He, *and she*, are the products of secrecy and sexual shaming and cross-wiring that is rampant in our world. *We cannot heal sexuality in the broadest way until all of us are willing to accept the truth about every one of us.*

If you would like to help, fill out the questionnaire that follows and mail it to me. You can help even if you have never been sexual with children. I need responses from people who have had no contact with children, those who have had sexual feelings but not acted on them, as well as those of you who had sexual contact.

If you choose to respond, I wish to thank you deeply for being involved in a project that is so painful to think about. Together, we can work to change our culture so children can grow up more safely.

IF YOU WILL HELP

If you would be willing to provide information about sexual feelings and activities to be used in a future book, please complete these questions and mail to me. I am very interested in your responses even if you have had few of the experiences I am asking about.

Questionnaire

1. ☐ Female ☐ Male

2. ☐ Coupled ☐ Married ☐ Divorced ☐ Single
   (check all that apply)

3. Age _____

4. ☐ Bisexual ☐ Heterosexual
   ☐ Homosexual ☐ Asexual

5. Was your religious upbringing ☐ strong
   ☐ moderate or ☐ minimal?

6. How many sex partners have you had? _____

7. How many hours (average) per week
   do you masturbate? _____

8. How many hours per week do you think about sexual
   or romantic activities? _____

9. Have you been sexual with: (check all that apply)
   ☐ babies ☐ children ☐ teen minors
   ☐ animals (what kind?)_____
   ☐ same sex ☐ over the phone
   ☐ over computers ☐ massage parlor ☐ prostitute(s)
   ☐ adult book store patrons ☐ married people ☐ with
   magazines or videos ☐ siblings ☐ parents or parent
   figure ☐ authority figures (teachers, religious people,
   gurus, employers, etc.) ☐ other (name) _____

Please describe these activities on a separate sheet of paper.
What did (do) you feel while being sexual? What did (do) you
think about? Also include numbers, occurrences and frequency
of items you check.

10. Have you had sexual feelings that you haven't acted on toward:
    ☐ babies ☐ children ☐ teen minors
    ☐ animals (what kind?) _____
    ☐ same sex ☐ over the phone
    ☐ over computers ☐ massage parlor ☐ prostitute(s)
    ☐ adult book store patrons ☐ married people ☐ with magazines or videos ☐ siblings ☐ parents or parent figure ☐ authority figures (teachers, religious people, gurus, employers, etc.) ☐ other (name)_____

Please describe these activities on a separate sheet of paper. What did (do) you feel? What did (do) you think about?

11. What was breast feeding like for you? Were you sexually aroused by it? Did you want the arousal for your pleasure? Use separate sheet of paper.

12. How many one-time sexual encounters have you had? (approximately)_____

13. What is your memory of your first sexual experience? (Any age from birth on). Use separate sheet of paper.

14. How was your sexuality abused? (this means sexually abused, shamed, or sexualized relationships in childhood or adult life) Use separate sheet of paper.

15. Are you in sexual recovery? _____ If yes, for how long? _____ On a separate sheet, describe how you are doing this, i.e. Twelve Step programs, therapy, etc.

16. Please describe any other sexual activities, preferences, and experiences that may be helpful to this study. Use separate sheet of paper.

17. What feelings come up for you as you complete this questionnaire? (i.e. shame, fear, disgust, aloneness, arousal, secrecy, etc.) Use separate sheet of paper.

Note: I would like to learn about the experience of men and women who are (or have been) sexual with young children, particularly babies. If you have had such experience, I would like to ask you to write out in detail what it is (was) like for you. What goes on (went on) in your mind before, during and after. Do (did) you prevent guilt feelings? If so, how? (Note that I am required to report the current abuse of children if I can identify you.)

Thank you for taking the time to tell your story. I will use it with respect.

SEX ADDICTS WITH SIGNIFICANT RECOVERY

If you have been involved in sexual recovery for several years, and have discovered what healthy sexual energy is like, I would like to hear your story, particularly your experience of sexual energy. If you are willing to be interviewed, please include your name, address and phone number. Thank you for your help in gathering information about this little-studied subject.

Are you willing to be interviewed? If you are, send me your name, address and phone number.

Send to:
Anne Stirling Hastings
Integrity Resources
P.O. Box 40083
Bellevue, WA 98005

Appendix 2

REQUEST FOR INFORMATION TO BE USED IN FUTURE BOOK
AMERICA'S SEXUAL CRISIS

America's Sexual Crisis will be published in late 1994. It will describe the desperate nature of sexuality in this culture, as well as what can be done to change our culture to allow for the emergence of healthy sexuality. If you would like to help with this book, I have included some questions. You can select some or all to answer.

The subjects I will discuss are reflected in the chapter titles below. I would appreciate reading your thoughts and experiences about any one or more of these subjects.

1. Healthy Sexuality: What It Really Is

2. Monogamously Bonding Creatures in a Healthy Culture

3. Healthy Jealousy

4. The Beginning of Bodily Shame—Pregnancy and Breast Feeding

5. Don't Talk About Sex: The Rule That Creates the Crisis

6. The Mating Dance Gone Awry: Sexual Harassment and Objectification

7. Advertisers Encourage and Exploit Unhealthy Cultural Attitudes

8. The Billion Dollar Sexual Services Industry

9. Sex Jokes: The Real Sex Education

10. Sex Addiction Is Supported by Our Culture

11. Most "Sexual Preferences" Are Not Healthy

12. "Sex Drive" Is a Cultural Artifact

13. Sex Therapy: Perpetuating Unhealthy Sexuality

14. Sex Therapy: The Fallacy of "Having Better Sex"

15. Sexual Abuse of Children Will Continue as Long as ASC's Are Not Allowed to Recover

I am especially interested in your breast feeding experiences. If you fed your baby from your breast, did you find it sexually arousing? Did you have orgasms? Some women masturbate while nursing. Did you want to? Did you want to be aroused when you fed your child? If you were aroused, how did you feel about that? Was it frustrating? Pleasurable? Shameful? Secret? Frightening?

Do you have a happy sex life? What is sex like? How does it begin, what happens next, and how does it end? Is it predictable? Has it changed from reading this book? Do you want it to change?

What changed for you from reading this book? What were the differences between you and your partner that lead you to read it, and was it helpful?

Do you feel that a moratorium is important to your sexual recovery? What about a moratorium from masturbation? What is making love to yourself like? Were you able to try it?

How much sex do you have? Disregard our culture's definition of "having sex," then write about your feelings of general
sexual awareness, of arousal, of sexual contact and also intercourse and orgasm. Include approximate frequency of each.

What does shame feel like? When does yours come up? Can
you recognize when your partner is feeling shame, or "in shame?"

Do you have sex jokes you can share with me? I will categorize
them for a chapter demonstrating how we use jokes to release
shame, express hostility and discuss sex even while accepting
prohibitions against doing so. How does it feel to write the joke
down, knowing I will be studying it instead of laughing?

Have you been to a sex therapist? Was the person helpful?
Harmful? Please tell the story.

Have you been filled with jealousy? What does it feel like?
What did you do with the feeling? Do you have ways to avoid
jealous feelings? When have you felt monogamous? When have
you felt non-monogamous? What is it like to love your mate, and
find yourself sexually attracted to another person or to body
parts or to people in TV commercials?

I would like to hear any other experiences you may want to
share. Thank you for your help with this project.

Please send comments and answers to:

Anne Stirling Hastings
Integrity Resources
P.O. Box 40083
Bellevue, WA 98005

Suggested Reading

I. Books About Sexual Recovery

Allen, Charlotte Vale, *Daddy's Girl*. Berkley Publications, 1984.

Bass, Ellen, and Laura Davis, *The Courage to Heal*. Harper and Row, 1988.

Carnes, Patrick, *Contrary to Love: Helping the Sexual Addict*.
   CompCare, 1989.

Carnes, Patrick, *Don't Call It Love*. Bantam, 1991.

Carnes, Patrick, *Out of the Shadows: Understanding Sexual Addiction*.
   CompCare, 1983.

Davis, Laura, *Allies in Healing*. Harper Perennial, 1991.

Earle, Ralph and Gregory Crow, *Lonely all the Time*. Pocket Books, 1989.

Engel, Beverly, *The Right to Innocence*. Jeremy Tarcher, 1989.

Fraser, Sylvia, *My Father's House*. Harper and Row, 1987.

Hastings, Anne Stirling, *Reclaiming Healthy Sexual Energy*.
   Health Communications, 1991.

Hunter, Mic, *Abused Boys: The Neglected Victims of Sexual Abuse*.
   Lexington, 1990.

Kasl, Charlotte *Women, Sex and Addiction*. Ticknor and Fields, 1989.

Love, Patricia, *The Emotional Incest Syndrome*. Bantam, 1990.

Miller, Alice, *Thou Shalt Not Be Aware: Society's Betrayal of the Child*.
   Meridian, 1986.

Schaef, Anne Wilson, *Escape From Intimacy*. Harper and Row, 1989.

Schnarch, David M., *Constructing the Sexual Crucible: An Integration of Sexual
   and Marital Therapy*, Norton, 1991.

Schneider, Jennifer P., *Back From Betrayal*. Hazelden, 1988.

II. Books About General Recovery

Beatty, Melody, *Codependent No More: How to Stop Controlling Others and
   Love Yourself More*. Harper/Hazelden, 1987.

Bradshaw, John, *Healing the Shame that Binds You*.
   Health Communications, 1988.

Farmer, Steven, *Adult Children of Abusive Parents*.
   Contemporary Books, 1989.

Forward, Susan, *Toxic Parents: Overcoming Their Hurtful Legacy and Reclaiming Your Life*. Bantam, 1989.

Goldberg, Herb, *The Hazards of Being Male: Surviving the Myths of Masculine Privilege*. Signet, 1977.

Goldberg, Herb, *The Inner Male: Overcoming Roadblocks to Intimacy*. Signet, 1988.

Goldberg, Herb, *The New Male Female Relationship*. Signet, 1983.

Goldberg, Herb, *The New Male: From Self Destruction to Self Care*. Signet, 1980.

Hendrix, Harville, *Getting the Love You Want*. Henry Holt, 1988.

Hendrix, Harville, *Keeping the Love You Find*. Pocket Books, 1992.

Lee, John, *I Don't Want to Be Alone*. Health Communications, 1990.

Mellody, Pia, *et al*, *Facing Codependence*. Harper and Row, 1989.

Miller, Alice, *For Your Own Good: Hidden Cruelty in Child-Rearing and the Roots of Violence*. Farrar, Strauss & Giroux, 1984.

Miller, Alice, *The Untouched Key: Tracing Childhood Trauma in Creativity and Destructiveness*. Doubleday, 1990.

Miller, Alice, *Banished Knowledge: Facing Childhood Injuries*. Doubleday, 1990.

Schaef, Anne Wilson, *Codependence: Misunderstood, Mistreated*. Harper and Row, 1986.

Schaef, Anne Wilson, *When Society Becomes an Addict*. Harper and Row, 1989.

Schainess, Natalie, *Sweet Suffering: Woman as Victim*. Pocket Books, 1986.

III. Ficiton Useful to Recovery

Bryant, Dorothy, *The Kin of Ata Are Waiting For You*, Random House, 1976.

Piercy, Marge, *Woman on the Edge of Time*, Fawcett, 1985.

About the Author

Anne Stirling Hastings, Ph.D., a licensed psychologist in private practice in Bellevue, Washington, is the author of *Reclaiming Healthy Sexual Energy*. She specializes in sex addiction and sexual abuse, and teaches classes and workshops on reclaiming healthy sexual energy. She is married to Rex Holt, a sculptor, painter and certified Rolfer, with whom she always wants the same kind and same amount of sex.

The Printed Voice
98 Main Street No. 538
Tiburon, CA 94920